Swedish

phrase book & dictionary

Contacting the Editors
Every effort has been made to provide accurate information in this publication, but changes are inevitable. The publisher cannot be responsible for any resulting loss, inconvenience or injury. We would appreciate it if readers would call our attention to any errors or outdated information. We also welcome your suggestions; if you come across a relevant expression not in our phrase book, please contact us at: **comments@berlitzpublishing.com**

All Rights Reserved
© 2018 Apa Digital (CH) AG and Apa Publications (UK) Ltd.
Berlitz Trademark Reg. U.S. Patent Office and other countries. Marca Registrada. Used under license from Berlitz Investment Corporation.

Twelfth Printing: May 2018
Printed in China
Editor: Helen Fanthorpe
Translation: updated by Wordbank
Cover Design: Rebeka Davies
Interior Design: Beverley Speight
Picture Researcher: Tom Smyth
Cover Photos: all images iStock and Shutterstock
Interior Photos: Kevin Cummins/APA 39,

51; Ming Tang Evans/APA 76, 100; David Hall/APA 96; iStockphoto 16, 146, 156, 161, 162,165, 173, 174; Lucy Johnston/APA 187; Julian Love/APA 1, 14, 18, 27, 57, 61, 87, 99, 109, 110, 112, 114, 117, 120, 122, 124, 128, 131, 140, 154, 170, 179; Frank Noon/APA 95; Jonas Overodder/Imagebank.Sweden.SE 90; Sylvaine Poitau/APA 103; Beverley Speight 52; Corrie Wingate/APA 89; Gregory Wrona/APA 93, 107

Distribution

UK, Ireland and Europe
Apa Publications (UK) Ltd
sales@insightguides.com
United States and Canada
Ingram Publisher Services
ips@ingramcontent.com
Australia and New Zealand
Woodslane
info@woodslane.com.au
Southeast Asia
Apa Publications (SN) Pte
singaporeoffice@insightguides.com

Worldwide
Apa Publications (UK) Ltd
sales@insightguides.com

Special Sales, Content Licensing, and CoPublishing
Discounts available for bulk quantities. We can create special editions, personalized jackets, and corporate imprints. sales@insightguides.com; www.insightguides.biz

Contents

Food & Drink

People

Leisure Time

Special Requirements

In an Emergency

Dictionary

Pronunciation

This section is designed to familiarize you with the sounds of Swedish using our simplified phonetic transcription. You'll find the pronunciation of the Swedish letters and sounds explained below, together with their 'imitated' equivalents. To use this system, found throughout the phrase book, simply read the pronunciation as if it were English, noting any special rules below.

The Swedish alphabet has 29 letters, the last three of which are the vowels **å**, **ä** and **ö**. Unlike English, the letter **y** is a vowel, meaning that Swedish has nine vowels. Swedish vowels are pure vowel sounds, as opposed to being a combination of two sounds (diphthongs) as they often are in English. Diphthongs occur only in dialects such as **Gotländska** (spoken on the island of Gotland), **Skånska** (spoken in the southern province of Skåne) and **Dalmål** (spoken in Dalarna, a province roughly in the middle of the country.)

Swedish has very consistent rules with respect to the sounding of individual letters, i.e. all the letters should be pronounced distinctly, even vowels and consonants at the ends of words. The Swedish language is often referred to as a 'musical' language due to the fact that the intonation and rhythm moves up and down, giving the language a musical quality. Despite this stress, pronunciation is quite consistent. Most words with two or more syllables have primary stress on the first syllable of the word, and this can be followed by a secondary stress on the second syllable. There are also a number of words with two or more syllables which do not have stress on the first syllable, but often on the last. Stress has been noted in the phonetic transcription with underlining.

Consonants

Letter	Approximate Pronunciation	Symbol	Example	Pronunciation
c	like s in sit	**s**	**cykel**	_sew_•kerl*
g	1. before o, å, a and u, like g in get	**g**	**gata**	_gah_•ta
	2. before i, e, ö and ä, like y in yet	**y**	**get**	yet
	3. after r and l, like y in yet	**y**	**borg**	bohry
j	1. soft, like y in yet	**y**	**jag**	yahg
	2. after r and l, like y in yet	**y**	**familj**	fah•_mihly_
k	1. before o, å, a and u, like k in keep	**k**	**katt**	kat
	2. before i, e, ö and ä, like ch in chew		**köpa**	_chur_•pa
q	like k in keep	**k**	**Blomquist**	_bloom_•kvihst
r	strong, almost trilled, r		**röd**	rurd
s	like s in see	**s**	**sitta**	_siht_•a
w	like v in very	**v**	**wennergren**	_vehn_•eh•_grehn_
z	like s in suit	**s**	**zebra**	_see_•bra

Letters b, d, f, h, m, n, p, t, v and x are pronounced as in English.
*Bold indicates a lengthening of the sound — emphasis on the vowel sound.

Consonant Clusters

Letter	Approximate Pronunciation	Symbol	Example	Pronunciation
ch	like sh in ship	**sh**	**check**	_shehk_
ck	like ck in tick	**k**	**flicka**	_flih•ka_
dj, gj, hj, lj	like y in yet	**y**	**djur**	_yeur_
sj, skj, stj, sch, ch	like sh in shop	**sh**	**sjal**	_shahl_
sk	1. before o, å, a and u, like sk in skip	**sk**	**skala**	_skah•la_
	2. before i, e, ö and ä, like sh in ship	**sh**	**skära**	_shai•ra_
tj	like sh followed by ch	**shch**	**tjock**	_shchohk_

Vowels

Letter	Approximate Pronunciation	Symbol	Example	Pronunciation
a	1. when long, like a in father	**ah**	**dag**	_dahg_
	2. when short, like a in cat	**a**	**katt**	_kat_
e	1. when long, like ee in beer	**ee**	**veta**	_vee•ta_
	2. when short, like e in fell	**eh**	**ett**	_eht_
	Approximate			

Letter	Approximate Pronunciation	Symbol	Example	Pronunciation
i	1. when long, like ee in see	**ee**	**bil**	*beel*
	2. when short, like i in bit	**ih**	**mitt**	*miht*
o	1. when long, like oa in coat	**oa**	**sko**	*sko**a***
	2. like the exclamation oh	**oh**	**font**	*fohnt*
u	1. when long, eu in feud	**eu**	**ruta**	*<u>reu</u>·ta*
	2. when short, like u in up	**uh**	**uppe**	*<u>uh</u>·per*
y	like ew in new	**ew**	**byta**	*b<u>ew</u>·ta*
å	1. when long, like oa in oar	**oa**	**gå**	*goa*
	2. when short, like o in hot	**oh**	**åtta**	*<u>oh</u>·ta*
ä	1. when long, like ai in air	**ai**	**här**	*hair*
	2. when short, like e in set	**eh**	**säng**	*sehng*
ö	1. when long, like u in cure	**ur**	**smör**	*sm**ur***
	2. when short, like u in nut	**uh**	**rött**	*ruhrt*

Swedish vowels are divided into two groups: hard and soft.
A, o, u and **å** are hard vowels; **e, i, y, ä** and **ö** are soft vowels.
Vowels can also be pronounced either long or short. When a vowel is
pronounced 'long' the sound is longer, but also more open and rounder.
The 'short' vowel sounds are more closed, literally a 'shorter' sound
than a long vowel. An easy rule to remember is that if the vowel is
followed by a single consonant, as in **stad** (city), it is long. If the vowel
is followed by a double consonant, as in **katt** (cat), the vowel is short.
The exception to this rule is with the consonants **m** and **n**.

Swedish is spoken throughout Sweden as well as in the
coastal regions of Finland and Estonia. While written Swedish
has been standardized, there are characteristic spoken dialects in
certain regions such as Gotland, Skåne and Dalarna. Other languages,
in addition to Swedish, are also spoken in Sweden, such as Finnish,
which is spoken in some communities in Northern Sweden, and the
Sámi (Lappish) languages, which are spoken in Sámi communities
throughout Northern Norway, Sweden, Finland and Russia. Swedish,
Norwegian, Danish, Icelandic and Faroese (spoken on the Faroe Islands)
are all derived from Old Norse, the language spoken prior to the Viking
Age. Over time, the Scandinavian languages developed from this
common language. Danish, Norwegian and Swedish are separate and
distinct languages but remain close enough that they are mutually
intelligible. The Finnish and Sámi languages belong to a different
language family, to which Hungarian also belongs.

How to use this Book

> Sometimes you see two alternatives separated by a slash. Choose the one that's right for your situation.

ESSENTIAL

I'm here on vacation [holiday]/business
I'm going to...
I'm staying at hotel/youth hostel.

Jag är här på semester/affärsresa.
yahg air hair poa seh·mehs·ter/a·fairs·ree·sa
Jag ska resa till... *yahg skah ree·sa tihl...*
Jag bor på hotell/vandrarhem. *yahg boar pao hoh·tehl/vahnd·rar·rehm*

> Words you may see are shown in YOU MAY SEE boxes.

YOU MAY SEE...

TULL	customs
TAXFRIA VAROR	duty-free goods
VAROR ATT FÖRTULLA	goods to declare

> Any of the words or phrases listed can be plugged into the sentence below.

Watching Sport

When's...?
  the basketball game

  the cycling race
  the golf tournament
  the soccer [football] game

När börjar...? *nair bur·yar...*
basketboll matchen
bahs·keht·bohl·ma·shchehn
cykeltävlingen *sew·kehl·taiv·lihng·ehn*
golfspelet *golf·spee·leht*
fotbollsmatchen *foat·bohls·ma·shchehn*

Swedish phrases appear in purple.

Read the simplified pronunciation as if it were English. For more on pronunciation, see page 7.

Personal

I'm...	**Jag är...** *yahg air...*
single	**ogift** *oa·yift*
in a relationship	**i ett förhållande** *ee eht furr·hoal·an·der*
married	**gift** *yihft*
divorced	**skild** *shihld*
separated	**separerad** *seh·pa·ree·rad*
I'm a widow/widower.	**Jag är änka/änkling.** *yahg air ehng·ka/ehngk·lihng*

For Numbers, see page 179.

Related phrases can be found by going to the page number indicated.

Swedes shake hands when greeting someone and when saying goodbye; this holds for meeting new people but is also often the case with colleagues or acquaintances.

Information boxes contain relevant country, culture and language tips.

Expressions you may hear are shown in You May Hear boxes.

YOU MAY HEAR...

Jag talar bara lite engelska. *yahg tah·lar bah·ra lee·ter ehng·ehl·ska*
I speak only a little English.

Jag talar inte engelska. *yahg tah·lar in·ter ehng·ehl·ska*
I don't speak English.

Color-coded side bars identify each section of the book.

Survival

Arrival & Departure

ESSENTIAL

I'm here on vacation [holiday]/business.	**Jag är här på semester/affärsresa.** *Yahg air hair poa seh•mehs•ter/a•fairs•ree•sa*
I'm going to...	**Jag ska resa till...** *yahg skah ree•sa tihl...*
I'm staying at a hotel/youth hostel.	**Jag bor på hotell/vandrarhem.** *yahg boar poa hoh•tehl/vahnd•rar•hehm*

YOU MAY HEAR...

Er biljett/Ert pass, tack. *eer bihl•yeht/ eert pas tak*	Your ticket/passport, please.
Vad är syftet med ert besök? *vahd air sewf•tet meed ehrt beh•surk*	What's the purpose of your visit?
Var bor du? *vahr boar deu*	Where are you staying?
Hur länge ska du stanna? *heur lehng•er skah deu stan•a*	How long are you staying?
Vem är du här med? *vehm air deu hair meed*	Who are you here with?

Border Control

I'm just passing through.	**Jag är bara på genomresa.** *yahg air bah•ra poa ye•nohm•ree•sa*
I would like to declare...	**Jag skulle vilja förtulla...** *yahg skuh•ler vihl•ya furr•tuh•la...*
I have nothing to declare.	**Jag har inget att förtulla.** *yahg hahr ihng•eht at furr•tuh•la*

YOU MAY HEAR...

Har du något att förtulla?
hahr deu noa•goht at furr•tuh•la
Du måste betala tull för det här.
deu mos•ter beh•tah•la tuhl furr dee hair
Var snäll och öppna den här väskan.
vahr snehl ohk urp•na dehn hair vehs•kan

Anything to
declare?
You must pay duty
on this.
Please open this bag.

YOU MAY SEE...

TULL	customs
TAXFRIA VAROR	duty-free goods
VAROR ATT FÖRTULLA	goods to declare
INGET ATT FÖRTULLA	nothing to declare
PASSKONTROLL	passport control
POLIS	police

Money

ESSENTIAL

Where's…?	**Var ligger…?** *vahr lih·gehr…*
the ATM	**bankomaten** *bank·oa·mah·tehn*
the bank	**banken** *bank·ehn*
the currency exchange office	**växelkontoret** *vehx·ehl·kohn·toar·eht*
What time does the bank open/close?	**När öppnar/stänger banken?** *nair urp·nahr/ stehng·ehr bank·ehn*
I'd like to change dollars/pounds into kronor.	**Jag skulle vilja växla dollar/pund till kronor.** *yahg skuh·ler vihl·ya vehx·la doh·lar/ pund tihl kroa·nohr*
I want to cash some traveler's checks [cheques].	**Jag skulle vilja lösa in några resecheckar.** *yahg skuh·ler vihl·ya lur·sa ihn noa·gra ree·seh·sheh·kar*

At the Bank

Can I exchange foreign currency here?	**Kan jag växla pengar här?** *kan yahg vehx·la pehng·ar hair*
What's the exchange rate?	**Vad är växelkursen?** *vahd air vehx·ehl·keur·shehn*
I think there's a mistake.	**Jag tror det är ett misstag.** *Yahg troar dee air eht mis·tagh*
How much is the fee?	**Hur mycket är expeditionsavgiften?** *Heur mew·ker air ehx·peh·dee·shoans·afv·yihf·tehn*
I've lost my traveler's checks.	**Jag har tappat mina resecheckar.** *Yahg hahr ta·pat mee·na ree·seh·sheh·kar*

17

YOU MAY SEE...

SÄTT IN KORTET	insert card
AVBESTÄLLA	cancel
RENSA	clear
ENTER	enter
PINKOD	PIN
TA UT	withdraw
FRÅN CHEKKONTO	from checking [current] account
FRÅN SPARKONTO	from savings account
KVITTOT	receipt

I've lost my card.	**Jag har tappat mitt kort.** *yahg hahr ta·pat miht koart*
My credit cards have been stolen.	**Mina kreditkort är stulna.** *mee·na kreh·deet·koart air steul·na*
My card doesn't work.	**Mitt kort fungerar inte.** *miht koart fuhn·gee·rar ihn·ter*
The ATM ate my card.	**Uttagsautomaten tog mitt kort.** *eut·tahgs·ah·toa. mah·tehn toagh mith koart.*

For Numbers, see page 179.

YOU MAY SEE...

Unlike the majority of other European Union countries, Sweden has not adopted the euro as its national currency. Sweden's monetary unit is the **krona** (singular) or **kronor** (plural) abbreviated to **SEK**.
The **krona** is divided into **öre**.
Coins: 50 **öre**, 1 **krona**, 5 and 10 **kronor**
Banknotes: 20, 50, 100, 500 and 1000 **kronor**

Cash can be obtained from a **Bankomat** (ATM) with MasterCard, Visa, Eurocard, American Express and other international credit cards or with a debit card. It is also possible to exchange traveler's checks in Sweden. In recent years, it has become quite common for the banks to refer customers with traveler's checks to the nearest **växelkontor** (currency exchange business) such as Forex or X-Change. These businesses are often located near or in points of departure/arrival such as airports or train stations, but can also be found in city centers. Remember to bring your passport with you for identification when you want to exchange money or cash traveler's checks. Most banks close at 3:00 p.m., though some are open later one day a week, often on Thursdays.

Getting Around

ESSENTIAL

How do I get to town? **Hur kommer jag till staden?** *heur koh·mehr yahg tihl stahd·ehn*

Where is...? **Var ligger...?** *vahr lih·gehr...*

the airport **flygplatsen** *flewg·plats·ehn*

the train [railway] station **järnvägsstationen** *yairn·vehgs·sta·shoa·nehn*

the bus station **bussterminalen** *bus·tehr·mee·nah·lehn*

the subway [underground] station **tunnelbanestationen** *teu·nehl·bah·neh·sta·shoan·ehn*

How far is it? **Hur långt är det?** *heur loangt air dee*

Where can I buy tickets? **Var kan jag köpa biljetter?** *vahr kan yahg chur·pa bil·yeht·tehr*

A one-way [single]/ round-trip [return]. **Enkel./Retur.** *ehng·kehl/reh·teur*

How much does it cost? **Hur mycket kostar det?** *heur mew·ker kos·tar dee*

Are there any discounts? **Finns det några rabatter?** *fihns dee noa·gra ra·bat·ehr*

Which gate? **Vid vilken gate?** *veed vihl·kehn gayt*

Which line? **Vilken kö?** *vihl·kehn kur*

Which platform? **Vilken plattform?** *vihl·kehn plat·fohrm*

Where can I get a taxi? **Var kan jag få tag på en taxi?** *vahr kan yahg foa tahg poa ehn tax·ee*

Please take me to this address. **Var snäll och kör mig till denna address.** *vahr snehl ohk churr may tihl deh·na ad·rehs*

Where can I rent a car? **Var kan jag hyra en bil?** *vahr kan yahg hew·ra ehn beel*

| I'd like a map. | **Jag skulle vilja ha en karta.** *Yahg skuh•ler vihl•ya hah ehn kahr•ta* |

Tickets

When is…to	**När går…till Uppsala?** *nair goar… tihl uhp•sah•la Uppsala?*
the (first) bus	**(första) bussen** *(furs•ta) buhs•ehn*
the (next) flight	**(nästa) flyg** *(nehs•ta) flewg*
the (last) train	**(sista) tåget** *(sihs•ta) toa•geht*
Where can I buy tickets?	**Var kan jag köpa biljetter?** *vahr kan yahg chur•pa bihl•yeht•er*
One ticket/Two tickets, please.	**En biljett/Två biljetter, tack.** *ehn bil•yet/tvoa bil•yeht•er tak*
For today/tomorrow. …ticket.	**Till dagens/imorgon.** *tihl dah•gens/ee•mo•ron* **…biljett.** *…bihl•yeht*
A one-way [single]	**En enkel** *ehn ehng•kehl*
A return-trip	**En retur** *ehn reh•teur*
A first class	**En första klass** *ehn furr•sta klas*
A business class	**En i affärsklass** *Ehn ee a•fairs•klas*
An economy class	**En turist klass** *ehn tuh•rihst klas*
How much does it cost?	**Hur mycket kostar det?** *heur mew•ker kos•tar dee*
Is there a discount for…?	**Blir det rabatt för…?** *bleer dee ra•bat furr…*
children	**barn** *bahrn*
students	**studerande** *steu•dee•ran•der*
senior citizens	**pensionärer** *pan•shoa•nair•ehr*
tourists	**turister** *tuh•rihst•ehr*
The express bus/ express train, please.	**Expressbussen/expresståget, tack.** *Ehx•prehs•buhs•ehn/ehx•prehs•toa•geht, tak*

The local bus/train, please.	**Lokalbussen/tåget, tack.** *Loh·kahl·buhs·en/ toa·geht, tak*
I have an e-ticket.	**Jag har en e-biljett.** *yahg hahr ehn ee·bihl·yet*
Can I buy a ticket on the bus/train?	**Kan jag köpa en biljett på bussen/tåget?** *kan yahg chur·pa ehn bihl·yeht poa bus·ehn/toa·geht*
Do I have to stamp the ticket before boarding?	**Ska jag stämpla biljetten innan jag går ombord?** *Skah yahg stehm·pla bil·yet·ehn·ihn·ahn·yahg·goar·ohm·bohrd*
How long is this ticket valid?	**Hur länge gäller denna biljett?** *Heur lehng·er yeh·lehr deh·na bihl·yet*
Can I return on the same ticket?	**Kan jag åka tillbaka med samma biljett?** *Kahn yahg oak·ha tihl·bah·ka mehd sam·a bihl·yet*
I'd like to…my reservation.	**Jag skulle vilja…min bokning.** *Yahg skuh·ler vihl·ya…mihn boak·nihng*
cancel	**avbeställa** *afv·beh·steh·la*
change	**ändra** *ehn·dra*
confirm	**bekräfta** *beh·krehf·ta*

Plane

Airport Transfer

How much is a taxi to the airport?	**Vad kostar en taxi till flygplatsen?** *Vahd kos·tar ehn tax·ee tihl flewg·plat·sehn*
To…Airport, please.	**Till…Flygplats, tack.** *tihl…flewg·plats tak*
My airline is…	**Mitt flygbolag är…** *miht flewg·boa·lahg air…*
My flight leaves at…	**Mitt flyg avgår klockan…** *miht flewg afv·goar kloh·kan…*
I'm in a rush.	**Jag har bråttom.** *yahg hahr broa·tohm*
Can you take an alternate route?	**Kan du köra någon annan väg?** *kan deu chur·ra noa·gohn an·nan vehg*
Can you drive faster/slower?	**Kan du köra lite fortare/långsammare?** *kan deu chur·ra lee·ter foar·ta·rer/loang·sam·a·rer*

YOU MAY HEAR...

Vilket flygbolag reser du med? _vihl•keht flewg•boa•lahg ree•sehr deu meed_ — What airline are you flying?

Inrikes eller utrikes? _in•ree•kehs ehl•er eut•ree•kehs_ — Domestic or International?

Vilken terminal? _vihl•kehn tehr•mee•nahl_ — What terminal?

Checking In

Where is check-in?	**Var är incheckningen?** _vahr air in•shehk•nihng•ehn_
My name is...	**Jag heter...** _yahg hee•ter..._
I'm going to...	**Jag ska resa till...** _yahg skah ree•sa tihl..._
I have...	**Jag har....** _Yahg hahr..._
one suitcase	**en resväska** _ehn rehs•vehs•ka_
two suitcases	**två resväskor** _tvoh rehs•vehs•kohr_
one piece of hand luggage	**ett handbagage** _eht hand •ba•gah•sh_
How much luggage is allowed?	**Hur mycket gratis bagage får man ha?** _heur mew•ker grah•tihs ba•goash foar man hah_

YOU MAY SEE...

ANKOMST	arrivals
AVGÅNG	departures
BAGAGEUTLÄMNING	baggage claim
INRIKESFLYG	domestic flights
UTRIKESFLYG	international flights
CHECKA IN	check-in
CHECKA IN E-BILJETT	e-ticket check-in
AVGÅNGSGATER	departure gates

Is that pounds or kilos?	**Är det i pund eller kilo?** *Air deht ee pund ehl•er cheeh•loh*	
Which terminal/ gate does flight… leave from?	**Vid vilken terminal/gate går flygnummer…?** *veed vihl•kehn tehr•mee•nahl/gayt goar flewg•nuhm•ehr…*	
I'd like a window/ an aisle seat.	**Jag skulle vilja ha en fönsterplats/plats i mittgången.** *yahg skuh•ler vihl•ya hah ehn furns•tehr•plats/plats ee miht•goang•ehn*	

YOU MAY HEAR…

Nästa! *nehs•ta*	Next!
Er biljett/Ert pass, tack. *eer bihl•yet/ eert pas tak*	Your ticket/passport, please.
Hur mycket bagage har du? *heur mew•ker ba•goash hahr deu*	How much luggage do you have?
Du har övervikt. *deu hahr ur•vehr•vikt*	You have excess luggage.
Det där är för tungt/för stort handbagage. *dee dair air furr teungt/furr stoart hand•ba•goash*	That's too heavy/ large for a carry-on [to carry on board].
Packade du väskorna själv? *pa•ka•der deu vehs•kohr•na shehlv*	Did you pack these bags yourself?
Har någon gett er något att ta med? *hahr noa•gohn yeht eer noa•goht at tah meed*	Did anyone give you anything to carry?
Töm era fickor, tack. *turm ee•ra fihk•ohr tak*	Empty your pockets, please.
Ta av er skorna, tack. *ta afv eer skoar•na tak*	Take off your shoes, please.
Nu är ni välkommna att borda flight nummer… *neu air nee vail•kohm•na at bohr•da flajt nuhm•ehr…*	Now boarding flight…

When do we leave/ arrive?	**När avgår vi/är vi framme?** *nair afv•goar vee/air vee fra•mer*
Is flight…delayed?	**Är det någon försening på flyg…?** *air dee noa•gohn furr•seen•ihng poa flewg…*
How late will it be?	**Hur försenat är det?** *heur furr•seen•at air dee*

Luggage

Where is/are…?	**Var finns…?** *vahr fihns…*
the luggage carts [trolleys]	**bagagekärrorna** *ba•goash•chair•ohr•na*
the luggage lockers	**förvaringsskåpen** *furr•vah•rihng•skoap•ehn*
the baggage claim	**bagageutlämningen** *ba•goash•eut•lehm•nihng•ehn*
I've lost my baggage.	**Jag har förlorat mitt bagage.** *yahg hahr furr•loa•rat miht ba•goash*
My baggage has been stolen.	**Mitt bagage har blivit stulet.** *miht ba•goash hahr blee•viht steu•leht*
My suitcase was damaged.	**Min resväska blev skadad.** *Mihn rees•vehs•ka bleev skah•dad*

Finding your Way

Where is…?	**Var finns…?** *vahr fihns…*
the currency exchange office	**växelkontoret** *vehx•ehl•kohn•toar•eht*
the car hire	**biluthyrningen** *beel•eut•hewr•nihng•ehn*
the exit	**utgången** *eut•goang•ehn*
the taxi	**taxin** *tax•een*
Is there…into town?	**Finns det…in till stan?** *fihns dee…ihn tihl stahn*
a bus	**en buss** *ehn buhs*
a train	**ett tåg** *eht toag*
a subway	**tunnelbana** *tuh•nehl•bah•na*

For Asking Directions, see page 35.

YOU MAY SEE...

PLATTFORM	platform
SPÅR	tracks
INFORMATION	information
BILJETTKONTOR	ticket office
ANKOMST	arrival
AVGÅNG	departure

Train

How do I get to the train station?	**Hur kommer jag till järnvägsstationen?** *heur koh•mehr yahg tihl yairn•vaigs•sta•shoa•nehn*
How far is it?	**Hur långt är det?** *heur loangt air dee*
Where is/are…?	**Var finns…?** *vahr fihns…*
the ticket office	**biljettkontoret** *bihl•yet•kohn•toar•eht*
the luggage lockers	**förvaringsskåpen** *furr•vah•rihng•skoap•ehn*
the platforms	**plattformarna** *plat•fohr•mar•na*
Could I have a schedule [timetable], please?	**Kan jag få en tidtabell, tack?** *kan yahg foa ehn teed•ta•behl tak*
How long is the trip?	**Hur lång tid tar resan?** *heur loang teed tahr ree•san*
Is it a direct train?	**Är det ett direkttåg?** *air deh•ta eht dihr•ekt•toag*
Do I have to change trains?	**Behöver jag byta tåg?** *beh•hur•vehr yahg bew•ta toag*
Is the train on time?	**Är tåget i tid?** *air toag•het ee tihd*

For Asking Directions, see page 35.

Departures

Which platform does the train to…leave from?	**Vilken plattform går tåget till…från?** *Vihl•kehn plat•fohrm goar tao•geht froan*
When is the train to…?	**När går tåget till…?** *nair goar toa•geht tihl…*

Statens järnvägar or **SJ** (the Swedish State Railway) operates an extensive network covering the entire country, while also offering international connections to Oslo, Copenhagen and Berlin. The X2000 train, which reaches speeds up to 200 km/h, serves many of Sweden's greater cities and towns. Long-distance trains have restaurant cars and/or buffets, and there are also sleepers and couchettes for both first and second class. The system is reliable and comfortable, and offers a wide range of travel options with respect to schedule and cost. Discount tickets are available for young children, families, students and senior citizens. Special travel cards and programs are also available. On some trains, marked **R** or **IC**, you must reserve a seat by purchasing a **sittplatsbiljett** in addition to your travel ticket. For extraordinary scenery, try the northern **Inlandsbanan** (Inland Railway) service, which runs from Mora in Dalarna to Gällivare beyond the Arctic circle. The **Vildmarksexpressen** (Wilderness Express) has old 1930s coaches and a gourmet restaurant, and runs on the same line between Östersund and Gällivare, with stops and excursions.

Is this the right platform for...?	**Är det här rätta plattformen till...?** *air dee hair reh·ta plat·fohr·mehn tihl...*
Where is platform...?	**Var är plattform...?** *vahr air plat·fohrm...*
Where do I change for...?	**Var måste jag byta till...?** *vahr mos·ter yahg bew·ta tihl...*

On Board

Can I sit here/open the window?	**Kan jag sitta här/öppna fönstret?** *Kan yahg sihta hair/urp·na fuhns·streht*
Is this seat taken?	**Är den här platsen upptagen?** *air dehn hair plats·ehn uhp·tah·gehn*
That's my seat.	**Det där är min plats.** *dee dair air mihn plats*
Here's my reservation	**Här är min bokning** *Hair air meen boak·nihng*

Bus

| Where's the bus station? | **Var är bussterminalen?** *vahr air bus·tehr·mih·nahl·ehn* |

YOU MAY HEAR...

Påstigning! *poa·steeg·nihng*	All aboard!
Biljetter, tack. *bihl·yet·er tak*	Tickets, please.
Du måste byta i... *deu moss·ter bew·ta ee...*	You have to change in...
Nästa hållplats... *nehs·ta hoal·plats...*	Next stop...

YOU MAY SEE...

BUSSHÅLLPLATS	bus stop
INGÅNG/UTGÅNG	enter/exit
STÄMPLA ER BILJETT	stamp your ticket

Public transportation in Sweden is an excellent and well-maintained system that includes **bussar** (buses), **tunnelbanan** (subways), **spårvagnar** (trams) and **tåg** (trains). All of these run frequently, usually between 5:00 a.m. and midnight on weekdays and a bit later on weekends. Most cities and towns have a bus system, though only a few have trams and subways. While it is possible to purchase single tickets for the different modes of public transportation, it is more cost efficient to purchase a card or set of tickets if you are going to be using a particular network frequently. Most major cities have websites that provide up to date information on routes, tickets and prices; many of the sites have English as a language option.

How far is it?	**Hur långt är det?** *heur loangt air dee*
How do I get to…?	**Hur kommer jag till…?** *heur koh•mehr yahg tihl…*
Does the bus stop at…?	**Stannar bussen vid…?** *stan•ar buhs•en veed…*
Could you tell me when to get off?	**Kan du tala om för mig när jag ska stiga av?** *kan deu tah•la ohm furr may nair yahg skah stee•ga afv*
Do I have to change buses?	**Behöver jag byta buss?** *beh•hur•vehr yahg bew•ta buhs*
Stop here, please.	**Stanna här, tack.** *sta•na hair tak*

For Tickets, see page 21.

Subway

Where's the nearest subway [underground] station?	**Var är närmaste tunnelbanestation?** *Vahr air nair•mas•ter tuh•nehl•bah•neh•sta•shoan*
Which direction?	**Åt vilket håll?** *Oat vihl•keht hohl*

The subway in Stockholm is efficient and easy to use. It runs from 5:00 a.m. to midnight on weekdays. Tickets are valid for one hour from the time they are stamped and can be bought from ticket booths; discount cards can be purchased from **Pressbyrån** (a newsstand). Tickets can also be purchased at **SL Centers**, some tourist offices and certain grocery stores. The public transportation websites will have information on these retailers and businesses and what types of tickets they sell. Day and multi-day cards are also available. Subway and bus tickets in Stockholm are interchangeable.

Can I have a map of the subway [underground], please?	**Kan jag få en tunnelbanekarta, tack?** *Kan yahg foa ehn tuh•nehl•bah•neh•kahr•ta tak*
Which line should I take for…?	**Vilken linje ska jag ta till…?** *vihl•kehn leen•yeh skah yahg tah tihl…*
Where do I change for…?	**Var måste jag byta till…?** *vahr mos•ter yahg bew•ta tihl…*
Is this the train to…?	**Är det här tåget till…?** *air dee hair toa•geht tihl…*
How many stops to…?	**Hur många hållplatser är det till…?** *Heur moh•ngah hohl•plat•sehr air deht tihl…*
Where are we?	**Var är vi?** *vahr air vee*

For Tickets, see page 21.

YOU MAY SEE…

LIVBÅT	life boat
FLYTVÄST	life jacket
ACTIVERA HANDBROMSEN	use parking brake
LÄMNA INTE VÄRDESAKER I BILEN	do not leave valuables in your car

Boat & Ferry

When is the car ferry to Gotland leaving?	**Hur dags går bilfärjan till Gotland?** *heur daks goar beel·fair·yan tihl goht·land*
Where are the life jackets?	**Var finns flytvästarna?** *vahr fihns flewt·vehs·tar·na*
Can I take my car?	**Kan jag ta med min bil?** *Kahn yahg tah mehd meen bihl*
Can I drive on to the ferry now?	**Får jag köra ombord nu?** *foar yahg chur·ra ohm bohrd neu*
What time is the next sailing?	**Hur dags går nästa?** *Heur daks goar nehs·ta*
Can I book a seat/cabin?	**Kan jag boka en plats/hytt?** *Kahn yahg boa·ka plats/hewt*
How long is the trip?	**Hur lång är resan?** *heur loang air ree·san*
Where should I park?	**Var ska jag parkera?** *vahr skah yahg par·kee·ra*

Taxi

Where can I get a taxi?	**Var kan jag få tag på en taxi?** *vahr kan yahg foa tahg poa ehn tax·ee*
I'd like a taxi now/for tomorrow at…	**Jag skulle vilja ha en taxi nu/imorgon klockan…** *yahg skuh·ler vihl·ya hah ehn tax·ee neu/ ee·mo·ron kloh·kan…*

Regular boat and ferry services, carrying cars and passengers, link Sweden to neighboring countries such as Norway, Denmark and Germany as well as to the U.K. Ferry services from Stockholm to the vacation destinations of Åland and Gotland in the Baltic Sea are very popular, as are ferries to Finland, Estonia and Latvia. Not to be missed are the ferry and steamer trips from Stockholm to the many surrounding islands, known as **Skärgården** (the Archipelago).

Taxis can be found at stands marked **Taxi**. You can also flag
down a taxi in the street, especially near hotels and bus and
train stations. Calling a taxi by phone is a third option; numbers are
available from your concierge or a local phone book. The sign **Ledig**
(free), when lit, indicates that the taxi is available.

Can you send a taxi?	**Kan du skicka en taxi?** _Kahn deu shih·ka ehn tax·ee_
Do you have the number for a taxi?	**Har du numret till taxi?** _Hahr deu nuhm·reht tihl tax·ee_
Pick me up at... (place/time)	**Hämta mig vid/klockan...** _hehm·ta may veed/kloh·kan..._
I'm going to...	**Jag ska resa till...** _yahg skah ree·sa tihl..._
this address	**denna adress** _deh·na ad·rehs_
the airport	**flygplatsen** _flewg·plat·sehn_
the train station	**järnvägsstationen** _yairn·vaigs·sta·shoa·nehn_
I'm late.	**Jag är sen.** _yahg air seen_
Can you drive faster/ slower?	**Kan du köra fortare/långsammare?** _Kan deu chur·ra fohrt·a·rer/loang·sam·a·rer_
Stop/Wait here.	**Stanna/Vänta här.** _sta·na/vehn·ta hair_
How much?	**Hur mycket kostar det?** _heur mew·ker kos·tar dee_
You said it would cost...kronor.	**Du sa att det skulle kosta...kronor.** _deu sah at dee skuh·ler kos·ta...kroa·nohr_
Keep the change.	**Behåll växeln.** _be·hoal vehx·ehln_
A receipt, please.	**Kvittot, tack.** _kvih·tot tak_

YOU MAY HEAR...

Vart vill du åka? _vart vihl deu oa·ka_	Where to?
Vilken adress? _vihl·kehn ad·rehs_	What's the address?

Bicycle & Motorbike

I'd like to hire…	**Jag skulle vilja hyra…** *yahg <u>skuh</u>·ler <u>vihl</u>·ya <u>hew</u>·ra…*
a bicycle	**en cykel** *ehn <u>sew</u>·kehl*
a moped	**en moped** *ehn moh·<u>peed</u>*
a motorbike	**en motorcykel** *ehn <u>moa</u>·tohr·<u>sew</u>·kehl*
How much per day/week?	**Hur mycket kostar det per dag/vecka?** *heur <u>mew</u>·ker <u>kos</u>·tar d**ee** pair dahg/<u>veh</u>·ka*
Can I have a helmet/lock?	**Kan jag få en hjälm/ett cykelås?** *kan yahg foa ehn yehlm/eht <u>sew</u>·kehl·<u>loas</u>*

YOU MAY HEAR…

Har du ett internationellt körkort? *hahr deu eht in·tehr·na·shoa·<u>nehlt</u> <u>churr</u>·koart*	Do you have an international driver's license?
Kan jag få se ert pass, tack? *kan yahg foa see eert pas tak*	May I see your passport, please?
Vill du ha en försäkring? *vil deu hah ehn furr·<u>sair</u>·krihng*	Do you want insurance?
Det blir en handpenning på… *dee bleer ehn <u>hand</u>·peh·nihng poa…*	There is a deposit of…
Underteckna här, tack. *<u>uhn</u>·der·tehk·<u>na</u> hair tak*	Please sign here.

Car Hire

Where can I hire a car?	**Var kan jag hyra en bil?** *vahr kan yahg <u>hew</u>·ra ehn beel*
I'd like to hire…	**Jag skulle vilja hyra…** *yahg <u>skuh</u>·ler <u>vihl</u>·ya <u>hew</u>·ra…*
a cheap/small car	**en billig/liten bil** *en bihl·eeg/lee·tehn beel*
a 2-/4-door car	**en bil med två/fyra dörrar** *ehn beel meed tvoa/<u>few</u>·ra <u>dur</u>·rar*

an automatic/ manual car	**en bil med automatväxel/ manuell** *ehn beel meed ah·toa·maht·vehx·ehl/ mah·nuh·ehl*
a car with air-conditioning	**en bil med luftkonditionering** *ehn beel meed luhft·kohn·dee·shoa·neer·ihng*
a car seat	**en bilbarnstol** *ehn beel·barn·stoal*
How much does it cost…?	**Hur mycket kostar det…?** *heur mew·ker kos·tar dee…*
per day/week	**per dag/vecka** *pair dahg/veh·ka*
per kilometer	**per kilometer** *pair chee·loh·mee·ter*
How much does it cost…?	**Hur mycket kostar det…?** *heur mew·ker kos·tar dee…*
for unlimited mileage	**för obegränsade mil** *furr oa·beh·grehn·sa·deh·meel*
with insurance	**med försäkring** *meed furr·sair·krihng*
Are there any special weekend rates?	**Har ni särskilda helgrabatter?** *hahr nee sair·shihl·da hely·ra·bat·ehr*

Fuel Station

Where's the next fuel station, please?	**Ursäkta, var är närmaste bensinstation?** *eur·shehk·ta vahr air nair·mas·the behn·seen·sta·shoan*
Fill it up, please.	**Fyll tanken, tack.** *feyl tan·kehn tak*
…liters, please.	**…liter, tack….** *lee·tehr tak*
I'll pay in cash/by credit card.	**Jag betalar kontant/med kreditkort.** *Yahg beh·tah·lar kohn·tant/meed kreh·deet·koart*

YOU MAY SEE…

VANLIG	regular
PREMIUM	premium [super]
DIESEL	diesel

Asking Directions

Is this the road to…?	**Är det här vägen till…?** *air dee hair vair·gehn tihl…*
How far is it to…?	**Hur långt är det till…?** *heur loangt air dee tihl…*
Where's…?	**Var ligger…?** *vahr lih·gehr…*
…Street	**…gata** *…gah·ta*
this address	**denna adress** *deh·na ad·rehs*
the highway [motorway]	**motorvägen** *moa·tohr·vair·gehn*
Can you show me on the map?	**Kan du visa mig på kartan?** *kan deu vee·sa may poa kahr·tan*
I'm lost.	**Jag har kommit vilse.** *yahg hahr koh·miht vihl·ser*

YOU MAY HEAR…

rakt fram *rahkt fram*	straight ahead
till vänster *tihl vehn·stehr*	on/to the left
till höger *tihl hur·gehr*	on/to the right
i/runt hörnan *ee/ruhnt hur·nan*	on/around the corner
mitt emot *miht ee·moat*	opposite
bakom *bah·kohm*	behind
bredvid *breh·veed*	next to
efter *ehf·tehr*	after
norr/söder *nohr/sur·dehr*	north/south
öster/väster *urs·tehr/vehs·tehr*	east/west
vid trafikljusen *veed tra·feek·yeus·ehn*	at the traffic light
vid avfarten *veed afv·far·tehn*	at the exit

YOU MAY SEE...

	STOPP	stop
	LÄMNA FÖRETRÄDE	yield
	PARKERING FÖRBJUDEN	no parking
	FARLIG KURVA	dangerous curve
	ENKELRIKTAT	one way
	INGEN INFART	no entry
	OMKÖRNING FÖRBJUDEN	no passing
	U-SVÄNG FÖRBJUDEN	no U-turn
	ÖVERGÅNGSSTÄLLE FÖR FOTGÄNGARE	pedestrian crossing

Parking

Can I park here?	**Får jag parkera här?** *foar yahg par·kee·ra hair*	
Is there a parking lot [car park] nearby?	**Finns det en parkeringsplats i närheten?** *fihns dee ehn par·kee·rihngs·plats ee nair·hee·tehn*	
Where's...?	**Var ligger...?** *Vahr lih·gehr...*	
the parking garage	**parkeringshuset** *par·kee·rihngs·huhseht*	
the parking meter	**parkeringsautomaten** *par·kee·rihngs ah·toa·mah·tehn*	
How much does it cost...?	**Hur mycket koster det...?** *heur mew·ker kos·tar dee...*	

per hour	**per timme** *pair tihm•er*
per day	**per dag** *pair dahg*
overnight	**över natten** *ur•vehr na•tehn*

Breakdown & Repair

My car broke down/ won't start.	**Min bil har gått sönder/startar inte.** *min beel hahr goat surn•dehr/star•tar in•ter*
Can you fix it today?	**Kan ni laga den idag?** *kan nee lah•ga dehn ee•dahg*
When will it be ready?	**När blir den färdig?** *nair bleer dehn fair•dihg*
How much?	**Hur mycket kostar det?** *heur mew•ker kos•tar dee*
I have a puncture/ flat tyre (tire)	**Jag har punktering** *Yahg hahr puhng•teh•rihng*

Street parking, parking lots and, in some cases, parking garages will be available in most of Sweden's cities and larger towns. Street parking is generally metered in city centers and downtown areas. A blue circular sign with a red slash tells you where parking is prohibited. There will be signs indicating whether or not parking is free. In places where parking is metered, a ticket allowing you to park for a specific period of time will need to be purchased. If this is the case, tickets can be purchased from a **biljettautomat** (ticket machine). You pay for the amount of time you want to park and then place the ticket on the driver's side of the car, on the dashboard, so that the ticket is in plain sight. In some cases, parking may be free, and there will be signs posted with time limits, usually two or three hours.

Accidents

| There's been an accident | **Det har hänt en olycka.** *dee hahr hehnt ehn oa•lew•ka* |
| Call an ambulance/ the police. | **Ring efter en ambulans/polisen.** *rihng ehf•ter ehn am•beu•lans/poa•lee•sehn* |

Places to Stay

ESSENTIAL

Can you recommend a hotel in…?	**Kan du rekommendera ett hotel i…?** *kan deu reh·koh·mehn·dee·ra eht hoh·tehl ee…*
I have a reservation.	**Jag har bokat rum.** *yahg hahr boa·kat ruhm*
My name is…	**Jag heter…** *yahg hee·tehr…*
Do you have a room…?	**Har ni ett ledigt rum…?** *hahr nee eht lee·dihgt ruhm…*
for one/two	**för en person/två personer** *furr ehn pehr·shoan/tvoa pehr·shoan·ehr*
with a bathroom	**med badrum** *meed bahd·ruhm*
with air-conditioning	**med luftkonditionering** *meed luhft·kohn·dee·shoa·neer·ihng*
For tonight.	**För ikväll.** *furr ee·kvehl*
For two nights.	**För två nätter.** *furr tvoa neh·tehr*
For one week.	**För en vecka.** *furr ehn veh·ka*
How much?	**Hur mycket kostar det?** *heur mew·ker kos·tar dee*
Do you have anything cheaper?	**Har ni någonting billigare?** *hahr nee noa·gohn·tihng bihl·ee·ga·rer*
When's check-out?	**När måste vi checka ut?** *nair mos·ter vee sheh·ka eut*
Can I leave this in the safe?	**Kan jag lämna detta i kassaskåpet?** *Kan yahg lehm·na deh·ta ee ka·sah·skoa·peht*
Could we leave our baggage here until…?	**Kan vi lämna vårt bagage här till klockan…?** *kan vee lehm·na voart ba·goash hair tihl kloh·kan…*
Could I have the bill/receipt, please?	**Kan jag få räkningen/kvittot, tack?** *Kan yahg foa rairk·nihng·en/kvih·toht tak*
I'll pay in cash/by credit card.	**Jag betalar kontant/med kreditkort.** *Yahg beh·tah·lar kohn·tant/meed kreh·deet·koart*

Somewhere to Stay

Can you recommend a hotel in...?	**Kan du rekommendera ett hotel i...?** *kan deu reh•koh•mehn•dee•ra eht hoh•tehl ee...*
a hostel	**ett vandrarhem** *eht vand•rar•hehm*
a campsite	**en kampingplats** *ehn kam•pihng•plats*
a bed and breakfast	**rum med frukost** *ruhm mehd fruh•kohst*
What is it near?	**Vad finns det i närheten?** *vahd fihns dee ee nair•hee•tehn*
How do I get there?	**Hur kommer jag dit?** *heur koh•mehr yahg deet*

At the Hotel

I have a reservation.	**Jag har bokat rum.** *yahg hahr boh•kat ruhm*
My name is...	**Jag heter...** *yahg hee•tehr...*
Do you have a room...?	**Har ni ett rum...?** *hahr nee eht ruhm...*
with a bathroom/ shower	**med bad/dusch** *meed bahd/deush*
with air conditioning	**med luftkonditionering** *meed luhft•kohn•dee•shoa•neer•ihng*
that's smoking/ non-smoking	**för rökare/icke-rökare** *furr rur•kah•rer/ ih•keh rur•ka•rer*
For tonight.	**För ikväll.** *furr ee•kvehl*

For two nights.	**För två nätter.** *furr tvoa neh·tehr*
For one week.	**För en vecka.** *furr ehn veh·ka*
Does the hotel have…?	**Finns det…på hotellet?** *fihns dee…poa hoh·tehl·eht*
a computer	**en dator** *ehn dah·tohr*
an elevator [lift]	**en hiss** *ehn hihs*
(wireless) internet service	**(trådlös) internet** *(troad·lurs) in·tehr·net*
room service	**rumservice** *ruhm·sehr·vihs*
a pool	**en simbassäng** *ehn sihm·ba·sehng*
a gym	**ett gym** *eht ym*
I need…	**Jag behöver…** *yahg beh·hur·vehr…*
an extra bed	**en extra säng** *ehn ehx·tra sehng*
a cot	**en tältsäng** *ehn tehlt·sehng*
a crib	**en barnsäng** *ehn bahrn·sehng*

For Numbers, see page 179.

For Numbers, see page 179.

YOU MAY HEAR…

Ert pass/kreditkort, tack. *ehrt pas/ kreh·deet·koart tak*	Your passport/credit card, please.
Kan du fylla i den här blanketten. *kan deu few·la ee dehn hair blan·keh·tehn*	Please fill out this form.
Skriv under här. *skreev uhn·der hair*	Sign here.

Price

How much per night/week?	**Vad kostar det per natt/vecka?** *Vahd kos·tar dee pair nat/veh·ka*

Does the price include breakfast/sales tax [VAT]?

Ingår frukost/moms i priset?
ihn•goar fruh•kohst/mohms ee pree•seht

Are there any discounts?

Ger ni rabatter? *Yehr nee ra•bat•ehr*

There is a wide range of places to stay in Sweden, from luxury to budget. Budget options include **privatrum** (private rooms), much like bed and breakfasts, or **stugor** (cabins) and **lägenheter** (apartments). Cabins and apartments are usually rented out on a weekly basis, but one- or two-night stays may also be an option. Information can be found at the local tourist office; you may also see signs along the road indicating that there is a vacancy in a cabin nearby. Motorists can look for **motel** (motels); these are reasonably priced with restaurants and car-friendly facilities. When looking for somewhere to stay in university towns such as Stockholm, Göteborg or Lund, staying at a **sommarhotel** (summer hotel) can be a good choice. Student dormitories are open to tourists in the summer and are a good option if you are traveling in a group. Families can enjoy a **familjehotell** (a family hotel), which has special rates for groups sharing the same room (three to six beds). These only operate during the summer months. All-inclusive accommodation is also available in the form of a **turisthotell** (tourist hotel) or **pensionat** (boarding house). These are clean and comfortable hotels or guesthouses that are often found at summer resorts and winter sport areas. Sweden also offers first class and deluxe hotels, usually found in larger cities and towns. Prices and amenities vary but the standards are usually high. Breakfast is usually included. When booking somewhere to stay during the summer months and high tourist season it is important to book in advance.

Preferences

Can I see the room?	**Kan jag se rummet?** *Kan yahg seh ruhm·eht*
I'd like a…room.	**Jag skulle vilja ha ett…rum.** *Yahg skuh·ler vihl·ya hah eht …ruhm*
better	**bättre** *beh·treh*
bigger	**större** *stuh·reh*
cheaper	**billigare** *bihl·ee·ga·rer*
quieter	**tystare** *tews·tah·rer*
I'll take it.	**Ja tar det.** *Yahg tahr deht*
No, I won't take it.	**Nej, jag tar inte det.** *Nay, yahg tahr deht in·ter*

Questions

Where's…?	**Var ligger…?** *vahr <u>lih</u>·gehr…*
the bar	**baren** <u>*bah*</u>*·rehn*
the bathroom [toilet]	**toaletten** *toa·ah·<u>leh</u>·tehn*
the elevator [lift]	**hissen** <u>*his*</u>*·ehn*
Can I have…?	**Kan jag få…?** *kan yahg foa…*
a blanket	**ett täcke** *eht <u>teh</u>·ker*
an iron	**ett strykjärn** *eht <u>strewk</u>·yairn*
the room key/ key card	**rumsnyckeln/nyckelkortet** *Ruhms·new·kehl/ new·kehl·koart*
a pillow	**en kudde** *ehn <u>keu</u>·der*
soap	**tvål** *tvoal*
toilet paper	**toalettpapper** *toa·ah·<u>leht</u>·pa·pehr*
a towel	**en handduk** *ehn han·deuk*
Can I use this adapter here?	**Kan jag använda den här adaptern här?** *kan yahg <u>an</u>·vehn·da dehn hair a·<u>dap</u>·tern hair*
How do I turn on the lights?	**Hur tänder man lamporna?** *heur <u>tehn</u>·der man <u>lam</u>·pohr·na*

YOU MAY SEE...

TRYCK	push
DRAG	pull
WC	restroom [toilet]
DAMTOALETT	women's restroom
HERRTOALETT	men's restroom
DUSCH	shower
HISS	elevator [lift]
TRAPPOR	stairs
TVÄTT	laundry
VAR GOD STÖR EJ	do not disturb
BRANDUTGÅNG	fire door
NÖDUTGÅNG	emergency exit
TELEFONVÄCKNING	wake-up call

Could you wake me at...? **Kan ni väcka mig klockan...?** *kan nee veh·ka may kloh·kan...*

Could I have my things from the safe? **Kan jag få mina saker från kassaskåpet?** *kan yahg foa mee·na sah·ker froan ka·sa·skoa·peht*

Is there any mail/a message for me? **Finns det någon post/eht meddelande till mig?** *fihns dee noa·gohn pohst/eht meed·deel·an·der tihl may*

Do you have a laundry service? **Har ni tvättservice?** *hahr nee tveht·sehr·vihs*

Problems

There's a problem. **Jag har ett problem.** *yahg hahr eht proh·bleem*

I've lost my key/ key card. **Jag har tappat bort min nyckel/mitt nyckelkort.** *yahg hahr ta·pat bort mihn new·kehl/ miht new·kehl·koart*

Throughout Sweden the current is 230-volt, 50-cycle AC. If you bring your own electrical appliances, buy a continental adapter plug (round pins) before leaving home. You may also need a transformer appropriate to the wattage of the appliance.

I've locked myself out of my room.	**Jag har låst ut mig ur rummet.** *yahg hahr loast eut may eur ruhm•eht*
There's no hot water/ toilet paper.	**Det finns inget varmvatten/toalettpapper.** *dee fihns ihng•eht varmt•va•tehrn/toa•ah•leht•pa•per*
The room is dirty.	**Rummet är smutsigt.** *ruhm•eht air smuht•siht*
There are bugs in our room.	**Det finns insekter på vårt rum.** *dee fihns ihn•sehk•tehr poa voart ruhm*
Can you fix...?	**Kan ni laga...?** *kan nee lah•ga...*
the air conditioning	**luftkonditioneringen** *luhft•kohn•dee•shoa•neer•ihng•ehn*
the fan	**fläkten** *flehk•tehn*
the heating	**värmen** *vair•mehn*
the light	**lampan** *lahm•pan*
the TV	**teven** *teh•veen*
the toilet	**toaletten** *toa•ah•leh•tehn*
I'd like to move to another room.	**Jag skulle vilja flytta till ett annat rum.** *yahg skuh•ler vihl•ya flew•ta tihl eht an•at ruhm*
...is/are broken.	**...är trasig.** *...air trah•sihg*

Checking Out

When do we need to check out?	**När måste vi checka ut?** *nair mos•ter vee sheh•ka eut*
Could we leave our	**Kan vi lämna vårt bagage här till**

baggage here until...?	**klockan...?** *kan vee lehm·na voart ba·goash hair tihl kloh·kan...*
Can I have an itemized bill/receipt?	**Kan jag få en specificerad räkning/ ett specificerad kvitto?** *kan yahg foa ehn speh·seh·fee·ee·rad rairk·ning/eht speh·seh·fee·ee·rad kvih·toh*
I think there's a mistake in this bill.	**Jag tror det måste vara fel på notan.** *Yahg troar dee mos·ter vah·ra feel poa noa·tan.*
I'll pay in cash/by credit card.	**Jag betalar kontant/med kreditkort.** *Yahg beh·tah·lar kohn·tant/meed kreh·deet·koart*

45

Renting

I've reserved an apartment/a room.	**Jag har bokat en lägenhet/ett rum.** *Yahg hahr boh·kat ehn lair·gehn·heet/eht ruhm*
My name is...	**Jag heter...** *yahg hee·tehr...*
Can I have the key/ key card?	**Kan jag få nyckeln/nyckelkortet?** *kan yahg foa new·kehln/new·kehl·koar·teht*
Are there...?	**Finns det...?** *fihns dee...*
dishes	**porslin** *poarsh·leen*
pillows	**kuddar** *keu·dar*
sheets	**lakan** *lah·kan*
towels	**handdukar** *han·deu·kar*

A service charge as well as **moms** (sales tax) is included in hotel and restaurant bills, but you are expected to round up a restaurant bill to the nearest **krona**. Tipping is generally not expected, but it's always appreciated if the service has been exceptionally good. It is customary to give a small tip to hairdressers, barbers, taxi drivers and porters.

utensils	**bestick** *beh·stihk*
When do I put out the bins/recycling?	**När ska jag ställa ut soporna/ återvinning?** *nair skah yahg steh·la eut soa·pohr·na/ oat·ehr·vihn·ing*
...has broken down.	**...har gått sönder.** *... hahr goat surn·dehr*
How does...work?	**Hur fungerar...?** *heur fuhn·geh·rar...*
the air-conditioner	**luftkonditioneringen** *luhft·kohn·dee·shoa·neer·ihng·ehn*
the dishwasher	**diskmaskinen** *dihsk·ma·shee·nehn*
the freezer	**frysen** *frew·sen*
the heater	**värmeelementet** *vair·meh·ehl·eh·mehn·teht*
the microwave	**mikrovågsugnen** *mik·roh·voags·eung·nehn*
How does...work?	**Hur fungerar...?** *heur fuhn·geh·rar...*
the refrigerator	**kylskåpet** *kewl·skoa·peht*
the stove	**spisen** *spee·sehn*
the washing machine	**tvättmaskinen** *tveht·mah·shee·nehn*

Domestic Items

I'd like...	**Jag skulle vilja ha...** *yahg skuh·ler vihl·ya hah...*
an adapter	**en adapter** *ehn a·dap·tehr*
aluminum foil	**aluminiumfolie** *ah·leu·mee·nee·um·foh·lyer*
a bottle opener	**en flasköppnare** *ehn flask·urp·na·rer*
a broom	**en sopborste** *ehn sop·borsh·ter*
a can opener	**en konservöppnare** *ehn kohn·serv·urp·na·rer*
cleaning supplies	**städutrustning** *staird·eut·reust·nihng*
a corkscrew	**en korkskruv** *ehn kohrk·skreuv*
detergent	**tvättmedel** *tveht·mee·dehl*
dishwashing liquid	**diskmedel** *disk·mee·dehl*
bin bags	**soppåsar** *sop·poa·sar*
a light bulb	**en glödlampa** *ehn glurd·lam·pa*
matches	**tändstickor** *tehnd·stih·kohr*

a mop	**en skurmopp** *ehn skewr·mop*
napkins	**pappersservetter** *pa·pers·sahr·veh·ter*
plastic wrap [cling film]	**plastfolie** *plast·foh·lyer*
a plunger	**en vaskrensare** *ehn vask·rehn·sa·rer*
scissors	**en sax** *ehn sax*
a vacuum cleaner	**en dammsugare** *ehn damm·seu·ga·rer*

For In the Kitchen, see page 83.

For Oven Temperatures, see page 186.

At the Hostel

Do you have any places left for tonight?	**Finns det några lediga platser ikväll?** *fihns dee noa·gra lee·dih·ga plats·ehr ee·kvehl*
Can I have…?	**Kan jag få…?** *kan yahg foa…*
a single/double room	**ett enkelrum/dubbelrum** *eht hng·kehl·ruhm/duh·behl·ruhm*
a blanket	**ett täcke** *eht tehk·er*
a pillow	**en kudde** *ehn keu·der*

If you are looking for something comfortable and reasonably priced, **Svenska Turistföreningen** or **STF** (the Swedish Tourist Club) is an excellent place to start. Here you can search for accommodations such as **vandrarhem** (youth hostels). If you are a member of **STF** or Hostelling International you get a member discount. Generally, room options include dormitory style rooms, split male and female, as well as smaller private rooms or family rooms. You are usually expected to bring your own towels and sheets as these usually are not provided, but can be rented. Shared kitchen facilities are often available, so that you can buy food at the local supermarket and prepare your own meals. Some hostels offer breakfast.

sheets	**lakan** _lah•kan_
a towel	**en handduk** _ehn han•deuk_
What time are the doors locked?	**När stängs ytterdörrarna?** _nair stehngs ew•ter•dur•ar•na_
Do I need a membership card?	**Behöver jag medlemskort?** _beh•hur•vehr yahg mehd•lehms•koart_
Here's my international student card.	**Här är mitt internationella studentkort.** _hair air miht in•tehr•na•shoa•nehl•ah stuh•dehnt•koart_

Going Camping

Can I camp here?	**Får man tälta här?** _foar man tehl•ta hair_
Is there a campsite near here?	**Finns det en campingplats i närheten?** _fihns dee ehn kam•pihng•plats ee nair•hee•tehn_
What is the charge per day/week?	**Vad kostar det per dag/vecka?** _vahd kos•tar dee pair dahg/veh•ka_
Are there...?	**Finns det...?** _fihns dee..._
cooking facilities	**kokmöjligheter** _koak•mury•lihg•hee•tehr_
electrical outlets	**nätuttag** _nairt•eut•tahg_
laundry facilities	**tvättmöjligheter** _tveht•mury•lig•hee•tehr_
showers	**dusch** _deush_
tents for hire	**tält för uthyrning** _tehlt furr eut•hewr•nihng_
Where can I empty the chemical toilet?	**Var kan jag tömma den kemiska toaletten?** _vahr kan yahg tur•ma dehn sheh•mihs•ka toa•ah•leh•tehn_

For Domestic Items, see page 46.

YOU MAY SEE...

DRICKSVATTEN	drinking water
INGEN CAMPING	no camping
INGEN GRILLNING	no barbeques
INGEN ÖPPEN ELD	no fires

Communications

ESSENTIAL

Where's an internet cafe?	**Var finns det ett internetkafé?** *vahr fihns dee eht ihn·tehr·neht·ka·feh*
Can I access the internet/check e-mail here?	**Kan jag komma ut på internet/kola e-post här?** *kan yahg koh·ma eut poa ihn·tehr·neht/koa·la ee·pohst hair*
How much per hour/half hour?	**Hur mycket kostar det per timme/halvtimme?** *heur mew·ker kos·tar dee pair tihm·er/halv·tihm·er*
How do I connect/log on?	**Hur loggar jag in?** *heur loh·gar yag ihn*
Can I have a phone card?	**Kan jag få ett telefonkort?** *kan yahg foa eht teh·leh·foan·koart*
Can I have your phone number?	**Kan jag få ditt telefonnummer?** *kan yahg foa diht teh·leh·foan·nuhm·ehr*
Here's my number/e-mail address.	**Här är mitt nummer/min e-postadress.** *hair air miht nuhm·ehr/mihn ee·pohst·ad·rehs*
Call me.	**Var snäll och ring mig.** *vahr snehl ohk ring may*
E-mail me.	**Skicka en e-post till mig.** *shih·ka ehn ee·pohst tihl may*
Hello. This is...	**Hej. Det här är...** *hay dee hair air...*
I'd like to speak to...	**Jag skulle vilja tala med...** *yahg skuh·ler vihl·ya tah·la meed...*
Repeat that, please.	**Kan du upprepa det, tack.** *kan deu uhp·ree·pa dee tak*
I'll be in touch.	**Jag hör av mig snart.** *yahg hur afv may snahrt*
Goodbye.	**Hej då.** *hay doa*
Where is the post office?	**Var ligger posten?** *vahr lih·gehr pohs·tehn*

| I'd like to send this to... | **Jag skulle vilja skicka det här till...** *yahg skuh•ler vihl•ya shih•ka dee hair tihl...* |

Online

Where's an internet cafe?	**Var finns det ett internetcafe?** *vahr fihns deht eht ihn•tehr•neht•ka•feh*
Does it have wireless internet?	**Finns det trådlös internet där?** *fihns dee troad•lurs ihn•tehr•neht dair*
What is the WiFi password?	**Vilket är WiFi-lösenordet?** *vihl•keht wai•fai•lur•sehn•oarde*
Is the WiFi free?	**Är WiFi:n gratis?** *air wai•fain grah•tihs*
Do you have bluetooth?	**Har ni blåtand?** *hahr nee bloa•tand*
How do I turn the computer on/off?	**Hur sätter jag på/stänger jag av datorn?** *heur seh•tehr yahg poa/stehng•her yahg afv dah•torn*
Can I print?	**Kan jag skriva ut?** *kan yahg skree•va eut*
Can I...?	**Kan jag...?** *kahn yahg...*
access the internet	**gå ut på internet** *goa eut poa ihn•tehr•neth*
check my e-mail	**kolla min e-post** *kohla meen eh•pohst*
plug in/charge my laptop/iPhone/iPad/BlackBerry?	**sätta i/ladda min laptop/iPhone/iPad/BlackBerry** *sehta ih/ladha meen laptop/iPad/BlackBerry*
access Skype?	**använda Skype** *an•vehn•a Skype*
How much per half hour/hour ?	**Hur mycket kostar det per halvtimme/timme?** *Heur mew•keh koh•star deht pehr halv•tihm•er/tih•mer*
How do I...?	**Hur gör man för att...?** *heur yurr man furr at...*
connect/disconnect	**koppla upp/koppla ner** *kohp•la uhp/kohp•la nehr*
log on/off	**logga in/ut** *loh•ga ihn/eut*
type this symbol	**skriva in det här tecknet** *skree•va ihn dee hair tehk•neht*

What's your e-mail?	**Vad har du för e-postadress?** *vahd hahr deu fu*rr *ee-pohst-ad-rehs*
My e-mail is…	**Min e-postadress är…** *mihn ee-pohst-ad-rehs air…*
Do you have a scanner?	**Har ni en skanner?** *Hahr nee ehn ska-nehr*

Social Media

Are you on Facebook/Twitter?	**Finns du på Facebook/Twitter?** *Fihns deu poa Facebook/Twitter*
What's your user name?	**Vilket användarnamn har du?** *Vihl-keht an-vehn-dar-namn hahr deu*
I'll add you as a friend.	**Jag lägger till dig som vän.** *yahg lehg-ehr tihl day sohm vehn*
I'll follow you on Twitter.	**Jag följer dig på Twitter.** *Yahg fuhl-yehr day poa Twitter*
Are you following…?	**Följer du…?** *Fuhl-yehr deu…*
I'll put the pictures on Facebook/Twitter.	**Jag lägger ut bilderna på Facebook/Twitter.** *yahg lehg-ehr eut bihl-dehr-na poa Facebook/Twitter*
I'll tag you in the pictures.	**Jag taggar bilderna.** *yahg ta-gar bihl-dehr-na*

YOU MAY SEE...

STÄNG	close
RADERA	delete
E-POST	e-mail
UTGÅNG	exit
HJÄLP	help
INSTANT MESSENGER	instant messenger
INTERNET	internet
LOGGA IN	login
NYTT MEDDELANDE	new message
AV/PÅ	on/off
ÖPPNA	open
SKRIV UT	print
SPARA	save
SKICKA	send
ANVÄNDARNAMN	username
LÖSENORD	password
TRÅDLÖS INTERNET	wireless internet

Phone

A phone card/prepaid phone please.	**Ett telefonkort, tack.** *eht teh·leh·foan·koart tak*
How much does it cost?	**Hur mycket kostar det?** *heur mew·ker kos·tar dee*
What's the area/ country code for…?	**Vad är riktnumret/landskoden till…?** *vahd air rikt·nuhm·reht/lands·koa·dehn tihl…*
What's the number for Information?	**Vilket nummer är det till Nummerbyrån?** *vihl·keht nuhm·ehr air dee tihl nuhm·ehr·bew·roan*
I'd like the number for…	**Jag skulle vilja ha numret till…** *yahg skuh·ler vihl·ya hah nuhm·reht tihl…*
I'd like to call collect [reverse the charges].	**Jag vill ringa ett mottagaren-betalar-samtal.** *yahg vihl rihng·a eht moh·tah·ga·ren be·tah·lar·sam·tahl*
My phone doesn't work here.	**Min telefon fungerar inte här.** *mihn teh·leh·foan fuhn·geh·rar ihn·ter hair*
What network are you on?	**Vilket nätverk använder du?** *vihl·keht neht·vehrk an·vehn·der deu*
Is it 3G?	**Är det 3G?** *air deht treh·geh*
I have run out of credit/minutes.	**Jag har inte mer pengar/minuter på kortet.** *yahg hahr ihn·ther meer pehng·ar/mih·nuh·tehr poa koart·eht*
Can I buy some credit?	**Kan jag fylla på kortet?** *kahn yahg fewlah poa koart·et*
Do you have a phone charger?	**Har du/ni en telefonladdare?** *Hahr deu/nee ehn teh·leh·foan·lad·ar·eh*
Can I have your number?	**Kan jag få ditt telefonnummer?** *kan yahg foa diht teh·leh·foan·nuhm·ehr*
Here's my number.	**Här är mitt nummer.** *hair air miht nuhm·ehr*
Please call me.	**Var snäll och ring mig.** *vahr snehl ohk rihng may*
Please text me.	**Var snäll och skicka ett sms till mig.** *Vahr snehl ohk shih·ka eht ehs·ehm·ehs tihl may*

YOU MAY HEAR...

Vem är det? *vehm air dee* — Who's calling?

Ett ögonblick. *eht ur•gohn•blihk* — One moment.

Tyvärr, är han/hon inte här. *tew•vair air hahn/hoan ihn•ter hair* — I'm afraid he/she is not in.

Han/Hon kan inte komma till telefonen. *hahn/hoan kan ihn•ter koh•ma tihl teh•leh•foan•ehn* — He/She can't come to the phone.

Vill du lämna ett meddelande? *vihl deu lehm•na eht mee•dee•lan•der* — Would you like to leave a message?

Ring tillbaka senare/om tio minuter. *rihng tihl•bah•ka see•na•rer/ohm tee•oah mih•neu•tehr* — Call back later/in 10 minutes.

Kan han/hon ringa upp dig? *kan hahn/hoan rihng•a uhp day* — Can he/she call you back?

Vad är ditt telefonnummer? *vahd air diht teh•leh•foan•nuhm•her* — What's your number?

I'll call you.	**Jag ringer dig.** *yahg rihng•ehr day*
I'll text you.	**Jag skickar ett sms till dig.** *yahg shih•kar eht ehs•ehm•ehs tihl day*

Telephone Etiquette

Hello. This is…	**Hej. Det här är…** *hay dee hair air…*
I'd like to speak to…	**Jag skulle vilja tala med…** *yahg skuh•ler vihl•ya tah•la meed…*
Extension…	**Anknytning…** *an•knewt•nihng…*
Speak louder/more slowly.	**Var snäll och tala högre/långsammare.** *vahr snehl ohk tah•la hur•greh/loang•sam•a•rer*

Can you repeat that?	**Kan du upprepa det?** *kan deu uhp•ree•pa d**ee***
I'll call back later.	**Jag ringer senare.** *yahg <u>rihng</u>•ehr <u>see</u>•na•rer*
Goodbye.	**Hej då.** <u>*hay*</u> *doa*

Fax

Can I send/receive a fax here?	**Kan man skicka/ta emot fax här?** *kan man <u>shih</u>•ka/ta ee•<u>moa</u>t fax hair*
What's the fax number?	**Vad är ditt faxnummer?** *vahd air diht fax•<u>nuhm</u>•ehr*
Please fax this to…	**Var snäll och faxa det här till…** *vahr snehl ohk <u>fax</u>•ah d**ee** hair tihl…*

Public phones take either **telefonkort** (phone cards) or **kreditkort** (credit cards). Phone cards are available at **Pressbyrån** (newsstand chain) and sometimes at independent newsstands. You can purchase a cell phone with a prepaid SIM card, something which is relatively cost efficient and worthwhile if you will be in Sweden for a longer period. Phone cards can also be used when dialing from any landline, e.g. at home of a friend or from a hotel. To call the U.S. or Canada from Sweden, dial 00 + 1 + area code + phone number. To call the U.K., dial 00 + 44 + area code (minus first 0) + phone number. Information on area codes for Sweden and international dialing codes can be found in the phone book and are usually available at hotels and youth hostels. The emergency number in Sweden is 112.

YOU MAY HEAR...

Fyll i tulldeklarationen, tack. *fewl ee _tuhl_-deh-klar-a-_shoa_-nehn tak*

Please fill out the customs declaration form.

Vad är värdet? *vahd air _vair_-deht*

What's the value?

Vad finns inuti? *vahd fihns _ihn_-eu-_tee_*

What's inside?

Post

Where's the post office/mailbox?	**Var ligger posten/postlådan?** *vahr _lih_-gehr _pohs_-tehn/_pohst_-loa-dan*
A stamp for this postcard/letter, please.	**Kan jag få ett frimärke till det här vykortet/brevet, tack.** *kan yahg foa eht _free_-mair-ker tihl dee hair _vew_-koar-teht/_bree_-veht tak*
How much does it cost?	**Hur mycket kostar det?** *heur _mew_-ker _kos_-tar dee*
I want to send this package by airmail/express.	**Jag vill skicka det här paketet med flygpost/express.** *yahg vihl _shih_-ka dee hair pa-_kee_-teht meed _flewg_-pohst/_ehx_-prehs*
The receipt, please.	**Kvittot, tack.** *kvih-toht tak*

Posten (the post office) is easy to find, just look for the blue **Post** sign with a yellow horn. Mailboxes are bright yellow. Business hours are 9:00 a.m. to 6:00 p.m. and until 1:00 p.m. on Saturdays. Like many other stores and business, you will need to take a number and wait for it to be called or displayed on a screen before you can be helped. Stamps can be purchased at **Pressbyrån** (newsstand chain) as well as some grocery stores.

Food & Drink

ESSENTIAL

Can you recommend a good restaurant/ bar?	**Kan du rekommendera en bra restaurang/pub?** *kan deu reh•koh•mehn•dee•ra ehn brah rehs•teu•rang/peub*
Is there a traditional Swedish/an inexpensive restaurant nearby?	**Finns det något värdshus/någon billigare restaurang i närheten?** *fihns dee noa•goht vairds•heus/noa•gohn bihl•ih•ga•rer rehs•teu•rang ee nair•hee•tehn*
A table for..., please.	**Ett bord för..., tack.** *eht bohrd furr...tak*
Could we sit...?	**Får vi sitta...?** *foar vee siht•a...*
here/there	**här/där** *hair/dair*
outside	**ute** *eu•ter*
in a non-smoking area	**vid bord för icke-rökare** *veed bohrd furr ee•keh•rur•ka•rer*
I'm waiting for someone.	**Jag väntar på någon.** *yahg vairn•tar poa noa•gohn*
Where are the toilets?	**Var finns toaletten?** *vahr fihns toa•ah•leh•tehn*
A menu, please.	**En meny, tack.** *ehn meh•neu tak*
What do you recommend?	**Vad rekommenderar du?** *vahd reh•koh•mehn•dee•rar deu*
I'd like...	**Jag skulle vilja ha...** *yahg skuh•ler vihl•ya hah...*
Some more..., please.	**Lite mer..., tack.** *lee•ter meer...tak*
Enjoy your meal.	**Smaklig måltid.** *smahk•lihg moal•teed*
The check [bill], please.	**Kan jag få räkningen, tack.** *kan yahg foa rairk•nihng•ehn tak*
Is service included?	**Är serveringsavgiften inräknad?** *air ser•veeh•rihngs•afv•yihf•tehn ihn•rairk•nad*

Can I pay by credit card?	**Kan jag betala med kreditkort?** *kan yahg beh‑tah‑la meed kreh‑deet‑koart*
Can I have the receipt, please?	**Kan jag få kvittot, tack?** *kan yahg foa kvih‑toht tak*
Thank you.	**Tack.** *tak*

Where to Eat

Can you recommend...?	**Kan du rekommendera...?** *kan deu reh‑koh‑mehn‑dee‑ra...*
a restaurant	**en restaurang** *ehn rehs‑teu‑rang*
a bar	**en bar** *ehn bahr*
a cafe	**ett kafé** *eht ka‑feh*
a fast-food place	**en grillbar** *ehn grihl‑bahr*
a steakhouse	**ett stekhus** *eht steek‑heus*
a cheap restaurant	**en billig restaurang** *en bihl‑eeg reh‑stah‑eu‑rahng*
an expensive restaurant	**en dyr restaurang** *ehn dewr reh‑stah‑eu‑rahng*

When it comes to eating out, there are many options, ranging from fast-food stands to five-star restaurants. If you are looking for a quick bite to eat, then a **gatukök** (fast-food stand) is an easy choice. If you are looking for more traditional cuisine, this can be found at a **värdshus** (roadside restaurant), **kafé** (cafe) or **restaurang** (restaurant).

Reservations & Preferences

I'd like to reserve a table...	**Jag skulle vilja boka ett bord...** *yahg skuh·ler vihl·ya boh·ka eht bohrd...*
for two	**för två** *furr tvoa*
for this evening	**till ikväll** *tihl ee·kvehl*
for tomorrow at...	**imorgon klockan...** *ee·mo·ron kloh·kan...*
A table for two, please.	**Kan jag få ett bord för två tack.** *kan yahg foa eht bohrd furr tvoa tak*
We have a reservation.	**Vi har bokat ett bord.** *vee hahr boa·kat eht bohrd*
My name is...	**Jag heter...** *yahg hee·tehr...*
Could we sit...?	**Får vi sitta...?** *foar vee siht·a...*
here/there	**här/där** *hair/dair*
outside	**ute** *eu·ter*
in a non-smoking area	**vid bord för icke-rökare** *veed bohrd furr ee·keh·rur·kah·rer*
by the window	**vid fönstret** *veed furns·treht*
in the shade	**i skuggan** *ee skuh·gan*
in the sun	**i solen** *ee sohl·ehn*

YOU MAY HEAR...

Har ni bokat? *hahr nee boh·kat*	Do you have a reservation?
Hur många blir ni? *heur moang·a bleer nee*	How many?
Rökare eller icke-rökare? *rur·ka·rer ehl·ehr ee·keh·rur·ka·rer*	Smoking or non-smoking?
Vill ni beställa? *vihl nee beh·steh·la*	Are you ready to order?
Vad vill ni beställa? *vahd vihl nee beh·steh·la*	What would you like?
Jag kan rekommendera... *yahg kan reh·koh·mehn·dee·ra...*	I recommend...
Smaklig måltid. *smahk·lihg moal·teed*	Enjoy your meal.

Where are the restrooms [toilets]?	**Var finns toaletten?** *vahr fihns toa·ah·leh·tehn*

How to Order

Excuse me!	**Ursäkta!** *eur·shehk·ta*
We're ready to order.	**Vi vill gärna beställa.** *vee vihl yair·na beh·steh·la*
May I see the wine list?	**Kan jag få se vinlistan?** *kan yahg foa see veen·lihs·tan*
I'd like...	**Jag skulle vilja ha...** *yahg skuh·ler vihl·ya hah...*
a bottle of...	**en flaska...** *ehn flahs·ka...*
a glass of...	**ett glas...** *eht glahs...*
a carafe of...	**en karaff...** *ehn kah·raf...*
The menu, please.	**En meny, tack.** *ehn meh·neu tak*
Do you have...?	**Har ni...?** *hahr nee...*
a menu in English	**en meny på engelska** *ehn meh·neu poa ehng·ehl·ska*
a fixed price menu	**en meny med fast pris** *ehn meh·neu meed fast prees*
a children's menu	**en barnmeny** *ehn bahrn·meh·neu*
What do you recommend?	**Vad rekommenderar ni?** *vahd reh·koh·mehn·dee·rar nee*
What's this?	**Vad är det här?** *vahd air dee hair*
What's in it?	**Vad är det i den?** *vahd air dee ee dehn*

Is it spicy?	**Är den kryddstark?** air dehn kreyd·stark
I'd like...	**Jag skulle vilja ha...** yahg skuh·ler vihl·ya hah...
More..., please.	**Lite mer..., tack.** lee·teh meer...tak
With/Without...	**Med/Utan...** meed/eu·tan...
I can't have...	**Jag kan inte äta mat som innehåller...** yahg kan ihn·ter air·ta maht som ih·neh·hoal·lehr...
rare	**blodig** bloa·dihg
medium	**medium** mee·dee·uhm
well done	**genomstekt** ye·nom·steekt
It's to go [take away].	**Jag ska ta den med mig.** yahg skah tah dehn meed may

For Drinks, see page 84.

YOU MAY SEE...

KUVERTAVGIFT	cover charge
FAST PRIS	fixed-price
MENY	menu
DAGENS MENY	menu of the day
DRICKS (INTE) INRÄKNAD	service (not) included
SPECIALITETER	specials

Cooking Methods

baked	**bakad** bah·kad
boiled	**kokt** koakt
braised	**bräserad** braeh·seeh·rad
breaded	**panerad** pah·neeh·rad
creamed	**rörd** rurd
diced	**i bitar** ee bee·tar
filleted	**filead** fih·leeh·ad

fried	**stekt** *steekt*
grilled	**grillad** *grihl·ad*
poached	**pocherad** *poa·sheeh·rad*
roasted	**ugnstekt** *eungn·steekt*
sautéed	**stekt** *steekt*
smoked	**rökt** *rurkt*
steamed	**ångkokt** *oang·koakt*
stewed	**stuvad** *steu·vad*
stuffed	**fylld** *fewld*

Dietary Requirements

I am...	**Jag är...** *yahg air...*
diabetic	**diabetiker** *dee·a·beh·tih·ker*
lactose intolerant	**laktosintolerant** *lak·toas·in·toh·leh·rant*
vegetarian	**vegetarian** *veh·geh·ta·ree·ahn*
vegan	**vegan** *veh·gahn*
I'm allergic to...	**Jag är allergisk mot...** *yahg air a·lehr·gihsk moat...*
I can't eat food	**Jag kan inte äta mat som innehåller...**
that contains...	*yahg kan ihn·ter air·ta maht som ihn·neh·hoa·lehr...*
dairy	**mejeriprodukter** *may·eh·ree·proh·duhk·tehr*
gluten	**gluten** *glue·tehn*
nut	**nöt** *nurt*
pork	**fläskkött** *flehsk·churt*
shellfish	**skaldjur** *skahl·yeur*
spicy food	**kryddad mat** *krew·dad maht*
wheat	**vete** *veeh·te*
Is it halal/kosher?	**Är det halal/kosher?** *air deht ha·lal/kosh·ehr*
Do you have...?	**Har ni...?** *hahr nee*
skimmed milk	**lättmjölk** *leht·myulk*
whole milk	**standardmjölk** *stahn·dardh·myulk*
soya milk	**sojamjölk** *soh·ya·myulk*

Dining with Children

Do you have a children's menu?	**Har ni en barnmeny?** *hahr nee ehn bahrn•meh•neu*
Can you bring a high chair, please?	**Kan jag få en barnstol, tack?** *kan yahg foa ehn bahrn•stoal tak*
Where can I feed/change the baby?	**Var kan jag mata/byta på babyn?** *vahr kan yahg mah•ta/bew•ta poa bai•been*
Can you warm this?	**Kan ni värma det här?** *kan nee vair•ma dee hair*

For Traveling with Children, see page 157.

How to Complain

How much longer will our food be?	**Hur länge till behöver vi vänta?** *heur lehng•er tihl beh•hur•ver vee vehn•ta*
We can't wait any longer.	**Vi kan inte vänta längre.** *vee kan ihn•ter vehn•ta lehng•rer*
We're leaving.	**Vi går nu.** *vee goar neu*
That's not what I ordered.	**Det här har jag inte beställt.** *dee hair hahr yahg ihn•ter beh•stehlt*
I asked for...	**Jag beställde...** *yahg beh•stehl•der...*
I can't eat this.	**Jag kan inte äta det här.** *yahg kan ihn•ter air•ta dee hair*
This is too...	**Det här är för...** *dee hair air furr...*
cold/hot	**kallt/varmt** *kalt/varmt*
salty/spicy	**salt/kryddat** *salt/krew•dat*
tough/bland	**segt/smaklöst** *sekt/smahk•lurst*
This isn't clean/fresh.	**Det här är inte rent/färskt.** *dee hair air ihn•ter reent/fairskt*

Paying

| The check [bill], please. | **Kan jag få räkningen, tack.** *kan yahg foa rairk•nihng•ehn tak* |

We'd like to pay separately.	**Vi vill betala var för sig.** *vee vihl beh·tah·la vahr furr say*
It's all together.	**Allt tillsammans.** *alt tihl·saa·mans*
Is service included?	**Är serveringsavgiften inräknad?** *air sehr·veeh·rihngs·afv·yihf·ten ihn·rairk·nad*
What's this amount for?	**Vad står den här summan för?** *vahd stoar dehn hair suhm·an furr*
I didn't have that. I had.	**Jag åt inte det. Jag åt…** *yahg oat ihn·ter dee yahg oat…*
Can I pay by credit card?	**Kan jag betala med kreditkort?** *kan yahg beh·tah·la meed kreh·deet·koart*
Can I have an itemized bill/ a receipt?	**Kan jag få en specificerad räkning/ett kvitto?** *kan yahg foa ehn speh·seh·fee·ee·rad rairk·nihng/ eht kvih·toh*
That was a very good meal.	**Det var en mycket god måltid.** *dee vahr ehn mew·ker goad moal·teed*
I've already paid	**Jag har redan betalat** *yahg hahr reh·dan beh·tah·lat*

Meals & Cooking

Breakfast

apelsin *a·pehl·seen*	orange
bacon *bay·kohn*	bacon
bröd *brurd*	bread
filmjölk *feel·myurlk*	thick yogurt
frukostflingor *fruh·kohst·flihng·or*	(cold) cereal
fruktjuice *fruhkt·yoas*	fruit juice
grapefrukt *grape·fruhkt*	grapefruit
gröt *grurt*	(hot) cereal
havregryn *hafv·reh·greun*	oatmeal

Frukost (breakfast) is usually served from 7:00 to 10:00 a.m.
Hotels and guesthouses offer a large buffet selection of cheese,
cold meat, bread, eggs, cereals and **filmjölk** (thick yogurt). **Lunch**
(lunch) is served from as early as 11:00 a.m. Although many Swedes
have a warm meal at lunchtime, some opt for a sandwich or a salad.
This is the best time to try the **dagens rätt** (specialty of the day).
Middag (dinner) is normally eaten early, around 6:00 or 7:00 p.m.,
though many restaurants continue serving until late, especially at
the weekend. Many Swedes will also eat a meal later in the evening,
referred to as **kvällsmål**; this evening meal usually includes
sandwiches, yogurt or soup.

honung _hoa·neung_		honey
kaffe... _ka·fer..._		coffee...
med mjölk _meed myurlk_		with milk
med socker _meed soh·ker_		with sugar
med sötningsmedel		with artificial
meed surt·nihngs·mee·dehl		sweetener
utan koffein _eu·tan koh·feen_		decaf
kallskuret _kal·skeu·reht_		cold cuts [charcuterie]
kokt ägg _koakt ehg_		boiled egg
korv _kohrv_		sausage
marmelad _mar·meh·lahd_		marmalade
mjölk _myurlk_		milk
muffin _muh·fihn_		muffin
müsli _mews·lee_		granola [muesli]
omelett _ohm·eh·leht_		omelet
ost _oast_		cheese
rostat bröd _roahs·tat brurd_		toast

småbröd _smoa_·brurd	roll
smör _smur_	butter
stekt ägg _steekt ehg_	fried egg
sylt _sewlt_	jam
thé _tee_	tea
vatten _va_·tehrn	water
yoghurt _yoh_·geurt	yogurt
ägg _ehg_	egg
äggröra _ehg_·rur·ra	scrambled eggs
äpple _ehp_·leh	apple

Appetizers

färska räkor _fair_·ska _rair_·kohr	unshelled shrimp [prawns], served with toast, butter and mayonnaise
förrätt _furr_·reht	appetizer [starter]
gravlax _grafv_·lax	marinated salmon
löjrom _lurj_·rohm	bleak roe, served with chopped, raw onions and sour cream and eaten on toast
rökt lax _rurkt lax_	smoked salmon
sill _sihl_	marinated herring
sillbricka _sihl_·brih·ka	variety of marinated herring
S.O.S. (smör, ost och sill) _ehs oa ehs_ (_smur oast ohk sil_)	a small plate of marinated herring, bread, butter and cheese
toast skagen _toast skah_·gehn	toast with chopped shrimp [prawns] in mayonnaise, topped with bleak roe
viltpastej _vihlt_·pa·stay	game pâté

Soup

buljong	beul·_yong_	broth
fisksoppa	fihsk·_sop_·a	fish soup
grönsakssoppa	_grurn_·sahks·_sohp_·a	vegetable soup
kall soppa	kal _sohp_·a	cold soup
kycklingsoppa	_chewk_·lihng·_sohp_·a	chicken soup
kött och grönsakssoppa		meat and vegetable
churt·oa·_grurn_·sahk·_sohp_·a		soup
köttsoppa	_churt_·sohp·a	a hearty soup of beef, vegetables and dumplings
löksoppa	_lurk_·sohp·a	onion soup
nyponsoppa	_new_·pohn·sohp·a	rose-hip soup
oxsvanssoppa	_oax_·svans·_sohp_·a	oxtail soup
potatissoppa	poa·_tah_·tihs·_sohp_·a	potato soup
rörd soppa	rurrd _sohp_·a	cream soup
sparrissoppa	_spa_·rihs·_sohp_·a	asparagus soup
spenatsoppa	speh·_nat_·sohp·a	a rich soup made from spinach, potatoes, milk and cream
tomatsoppa	toa·_maht_·soh·pa	tomato soup
ärtsoppa	_airt_·sohp·a	green or yellow pea soup

Fish & Seafood

abborre	_ah_·bohr·er	perch
ansjovis	an·_shoa_·vees	anchovy
blåmussla	_bloa_·muhs·la	blue mussel
braxen	_brak_·sehn	sea bream
böckling	_burk_·lihng	smoked Baltic herring
fisk	fihsk	fish
forell	foa·_rehl_	trout
färska räkor	_fairs_·ka _rair_·kohr	unshelled shrimp [prawns]

gravlax _grafv·lax_	marinated salmon
gädda _yeh·da_	sea perch
halstrad fisk _hal·strahd fihsk_	grilled fish
halstrad forell med färskpotatis _hal·strad foa·rehl med fairsk·poa·tah·tihs_	grilled trout with new potatoes
havsabborre _hafs·a·boh·rer_	sea bass
hummer _huhm·ehr_	lobster
hälleflundra _heh·leh·fleun·dra_	halibut
inlagd sill _ihn·lagd sil_	marinated (pickled) herring
Janssons frestelse _yahn·sons frehs·tehl·ser_	casserole with potatoes and anchovies
kammussla _kam·muhs·la_	scallop
kolja _kohl·ya_	haddock
krabba _kra·ba_	crab
kräfta _krehf·ta_	crayfish
kummel _keu·mel_	hake
lax _lax_	salmon
löjrom _lury·rohm_	bleak roe with chopped, raw onions and sour cream; served on toast
makrill _mak·rihl_	mackerel
marulk _mahr·eulk_	monkfish
matjesill _ma·shcheh·sihl_	marinated herring
multe _muhl·ter_	mullet
mussla _muhs·la_	mussel
mört _murt_	roach (type of fish)
ostron _oas·tron_	oyster
piggvar _pihg·vahr_	turbot
rimmad lax med stuvad potatis _rihm·ahd lax meed steu·vad poa·tah·tihs_	lightly salted salmon with creamed potatoes and dill
rocka _roh·ka_	ray (type of fish)

räkor _rair·kohr_	shrimp [prawns]
röding _rur·dihng_	char
rödspätta _rurd·speh·ta_	plaice
rökt fisk _rurkt fisk_	smoked fish
rökt lax _rurkt lax_	smoked salmon
rökt ål _rurkt oal_	smoked eel
sardin _sar·deen_	sardine
sill _sihl_	herring
sillbricka _sihl·brih·ka_	variety of marinated herring
sillsallad _sihl·sal·ad_	beet and herring salad
sjötunga _sjur·tuhng·a_	sole
skaldjur _skahl·yeur_	shellfish
skaldjurssallad _skahl·yeurs·sal·ad_	shellfish salad
skarpsill _skarp·sihl_	herring
småsill _smoa·sihl_	herring
S.O.S. (smör, ost och sill) _ehs oa ehs (smur oast ohk sihl)_	small plate of marinated herring, bread, butter and cheese
stekt fisk _steekt fisk_	fried fish
strömming _struhrm·ihng_	sprats (small Baltic herring) filleted and sandwiched in pairs with dill and butter in the middle
strömmingsflundra _strurm·ihngs·fleun·dra_	Baltic herring, filleted and sandwiched in pairs, fried, with dill and butter filling
stuvad abborre _steu·vad a·boh·rer_	perch poached with onion, parsley and lemon
tonfisk _toan·fihsk_	tuna
torsk _tohrshk_	cod
ugnsbakad fisk _eungns·bah·kad fihsk_	oven-baked fish

vitling <u>veet</u>·lihng	whiting
västkustsallad <u>vehst</u>·kuhst·<u>sal</u>·ad	west coast salad, with shrimp [prawns] and mussels
ål oal	eel
ångkokt fisk <u>oang</u>·koakt fisk	steamed fish

Meat & Poultry

anka <u>ang</u>·ka	duck
bacon <u>bay</u>·kon	bacon
biffkött bihf·churt	beef
biffstek bihf·steek	steak
bog boag	shoulder (cut of meat)
broiler <u>broy</u>·lehr	spring chicken
entrecote an·treh·<u>koat</u>	sirloin steak
falukorv <u>fah</u>·leu·kohrv	lightly spiced sausage
fasan fa·<u>sahn</u>	pheasant
filé fih·<u>leh</u>	filet mignon
fläsk flehsk	pork
fläskben <u>flehsk</u>·been	ham bone
fläskfilé <u>flehsk</u>·fih·<u>leh</u>	fillet of pork
fläskkarré <u>flehsk</u>·ka·<u>reh</u>	pork loin
fläskkorv <u>flehsk</u>·kohrv	spicy, boiled pork sausage
fläsklägg <u>flehsk</u>·lehg	knuckle of pork
fågel <u>foa</u>·gehl	poultry
får foar	mutton
get yeet	kid (goat)
grillad kyckling <u>grihl</u>·ahd <u>chewk</u>·lihng	grilled chicken
gås goas	goose
hamburgare <u>ham</u>·beur·ya·rer	hamburger
hare <u>hah</u>·rer	rabbit
hjort yohrt	deer

isterband _ihs_·tehr·band — sausage of pork, barley and beef

kalkon kal·_koan_ — turkey
kallskuret _kal_·skeu·reht — cold cuts [charcuterie]
kalops ka·_lohps_ — beef stew
kalvkött _kalv_·churt — veal
kalvsylta _kalv_·sewl·ta — cold veal in jelly
karré ka·_reh_ — tenderloin
kokt skinka koakt _shihng_·ka — boiled ham
korv kohrv — sausage
kotlett koht·_lehtt_ — cutlet
kyckling _chewk_·lihng — chicken
kycklingbröst _chewk_·lihng·brurst — chicken breast
kycklinglever _chewk_·lihng·lee·vehr — chicken liver
kåldomar med gräddsås och lingon — chopped [minced] meat and rice stuffed in cabbage leaves
koal·dohl·mar meed _grehd_·**soas** ohk _lihng_·ohn
kött churt — meat
köttbulle _churt_·buh·ler — meatball
köttfärs _churt_·fairs — chopped [minced] beef
lamm lamm — lamb
lammgryta _lamm_·gr**ew**·ta — lamb stew
lever _lee_·vehr — liver
leverpastej _lee_·vehr pa·_stay_ — liver pâté
lägg lehg — shank (top of leg)
lövbiff _lurv_·bihf — fried, thinly sliced beef, with onions

medaljong meh·dal·_yong_ — small fillet of cut meat
njure _ny**eu**_·rer — kidney
nötkött _nurt_·churt — red meat
oxkött _oax_·churt — ox
oxrullad oax·reu·_lahd_ — braised roll of beef

oxsvans _oax_·svans	oxtail
pannbiff _pan_·bihf	beef patty
prinskorv _prihns_·kohrv	small pork sausage
pärlhöns _pairl_·hurns	guinea fowl
ragu ra·_guh_	beef stew
rapphöna _rap_·h_ur_na	partridge
ren reen	reindeer
renstek med svampsås _reen_·steek meed _svamp_·s_oa_s	roast reindeer with mushroom sauce
revbensspjäll _reev_·beens·spehl	spareribs
rostbiff _rohst_·bihf	roast beef
rumpstek _ruhmp_·steek	rump steak
rådjur _roa_·yeur	venison
rådjursstek _roa_·yeur·steek	roast of venison
rökt renstek _rur_kt _reen_·steek	smoked reindeer
rökt skinka _rur_kt shihng·ka	smoked ham
sadel _sah_·dehl	saddle (cut of meat)
salamikorv sa·lah·_mee_·kohrv	salami
schnitzel _shniht_·sehl	escallope
sillsallad _sihl_·sal·ad	beet and herring salad
sjömansbiff _shur_·mans·_bihf_	casserole of fried beef, onions and potatoes, braised in beer
skinka shihng·ka	ham
spädgris _spaird_·grees	an unweaned piglet
stekt kyckling steekt _chewk_·lihng	fried chicken (not breaded)
T-benstek _tee_·been·steek	T-bone steak
tunga _tuhng_·a	tongue (cow)
ugnsstekt kyckling _eungn_·steekt _chewk_·lihng	roast chicken
vaktel _vak_·tehl	quail
varmkorv _varm_·kohrv	hot dog
wienerschnitzel _vee_·nehr·shniht·sehl	breaded veal cutlet

If you've never heard of typical Swedish food, you may at least be familiar with the famous **smörgåsbord** — it is a buffet meal on a grand scale, presented on a large, beautifully decorated table. You start at one end of the table, usually the one with the cold seafood dishes, marinated herring, **Janssons frestelse** (literally, Jansson's temptation, a potato and anchovies casserole) and salad. Then you work your way through the cold meat, meatballs, sausage, omelets and vegetables. Finally, you end at the cheeseboard and desserts. You're welcome to start all over again; the price is set, and you can eat as much as you like. You will find that the Swedes tend to drink **akvavit** (aquavit) or beer with the feast, although an accompanying glass of wine is becoming more common for those who find **akvavit** too strong. At Christmas time, the **smörgåsbord** becomes a **julbord** (Christmas buffet), popular in homes and restaurants alike.

vildand _vihld·and_	wild duck
vilt _vihlt_	game
älg _ehly_	moose
älgfilé _ehly·fih·leh_	fillet of moose
älgstek _ehly·steek_	moose roast
älgstek med svampsås _ehly·steek meed svamp·soas_	roast moose with mushroom sauce

Vegetables & Staples

avokado _a·voh·kah·doa_	avocado
basilika _ba·sih·lee·ka_	basil
blandsallad _bland·sal·ad_	mixed salad
blomkål _bloam·koal_	cauliflower
bouquet garni _boh·keh gar·nee_	mixed herbs

böna... *bur·na...*		...bean
bond *boand*		broad
bryt *brewt*		kidney
grön *grurn*		green
vax *vax*		butter
broccoli *broh·koh·lee*		broccoli
brysselkål *brew·sehl·koal*		Brussel sprout
bröd *brurd*		bread
bönskott *burn·skoht*		bean sprout
champinjon *sham·pihn·yoan*		mushroom
chilipeppar *shee·lih·peh·par*		chili pepper
dragon *dra·goan*		tarragon
endiv *an·deev*		endive
fullkornsmjöl *fuhl·kohrns·myurl*		whole wheat flour
fänkål *fehn·koal*		fennel
färskpotatis *fairsk·poa·tah·this*		new potato
gräslök *grairs·lurk*		chive
grön paprika *grurn pah·pree·ka*		green pepper
grönsak *grurn·sahk*		vegetable
grönsallad *grurn·sal·ad*		lettuce
gurka *geur·ka*		cucumber
haricots verts *ar·ee·koh·vair*		green bean
honung *hoa·neung*		honey
ingefära *ih·ng·eh·fai·ra*		ginger
kanel *ka·neel*		cinnamon
kantarell *kan·ta·rehl*		chanterelle mushroom
kapris *ka·prees*		caper
kikärta *cheek·air·ta*		chickpea
kokt potatis *koakt poa·tah·tihs*		boiled potato
kronärtskocka *kroan·airts·koh·ka*		artichoke
kryddpeppar *krewd·peh·par*		allspice

kummin _keu_•_meen_	caraway
kål _koal_	cabbage
kålrot _koal_•roht	turnip
källkrasse _chehl_•kra•ser	watercress
körvel _chur_•vehl	chervil
lagerblad _lah_•gehr•blahd	bay leaf
lins _lihns_	lentil
lök _lurk_	onion
majs _mays_	sweet corn
mjöl _myurl_	flour
morot _moa_•roht	carrot
muskot _muhs_•koht	nutmeg
mynta _mewn_•ta	mint (herb)
nejlika _nay_•lih•ka	clove
nudel _neu_•dehl	noodle
olja och vinäger _oal_•ya ohk vee•_nai_•gehr	oil and vinegar
palsternacka _pal_•stehr•na•ka	parsnip
paprika _pah_•prih•ka	pepper (fresh)
pasta _pas_•ta	pasta
persilja pair•_shihl_•ya	parsley
potatis poa•_tah_•tihs	potato

potatissallad *poa·tah·tihs·sal·ad*	potato salad
pumpa *puhm·pa*	pumpkin
purjolök *peur·yoh·lurk*	leek
ris *rees*	rice
rosmarin *roas·ma·reen*	rosemary
rova *roa·va*	turnip
rädisa *raid·dih·sa*	radish
röd paprika *rurd pah·pree·ka*	sweet red pepper
rödbeta *rurd·bee·ta*	beet
rödkål *rurd·koal*	red cabbage
salladshuvud *sal·ads·heu·vuhd*	head of lettuce
saltgurka *salt·geur·ka*	salted, pickled gherkin
salvia *sal·vee·a*	sage
schalottenlök *sha·loh·tehn·lurk*	shallot [spring onion]
selleri *seh·leh·ree*	celery
sirap *seh·rap*	syrup
skogssvamp *skoags·svamp*	field mushroom
smör *smurr*	butter
sockerärta *soh·kehr·air·ta*	sugar snap pea [mangetout]
sparris *spar·ihs*	asparagus
spenat *speh·naht*	spinach
squash *skoawsh*	squash (vegetable)
svamp *svamp*	mushroom
sötpotatis *surt·poa·tah·tihs*	sweet potato
timjan *tihm·yan*	thyme
tomat *toa·maht*	tomato
tomater och lök *toa·mah·ter ohk lurk*	tomato and onion salad
vanilj *va·nihly*	vanilla
vattenkrasse *kra·ser*	watercress
vetemjöl *vee·teh·mjurl*	wheat flour (regular)
vild champinjon *vihl·da sham·pihn·yoan*	wild mushroom

vitkål _veet_·k_oal_	white cabbage
vitlök _veet_·l_urk_	garlic
vårlök _voar_·l_urk_	shallot [spring onion]
zucchini seu·k_ee_·nee	zucchini [courgette]
äggplanta _ehg_·plan·ta	eggplant [aubergine]
ärta _air_·ta	peas
ättiksgurka _eh_·tiks·g_eur_·kah	pickled gherkin

Fruit

ananas _an_·a·nas	pineapple
apelsin a·pehl·_seen_	orange
aprikos a·prih·k_oas_	apricot
banan ba·n_ahn_	banana
bigarrå bih·ga·r_oa_	sweet morello cherry
björnbär b_yurn_·bair	blackberry
blå vindruva b_loa_ veen·dr_eu_·va	black grape
blåbär b_loa_·bair	blueberry
citron see·_troan_	lemon
dadel _dahd_·ehl	date
enbär _een_·bair	juniper berry
fikon _fee_·kohn	fig
frukt fruhkt	fruit
grapefrukt _grape_·fruhkt	grapefruit
grön vindruva _grurn_ veen·dr_eu_·va	green grape
hallon _hal_·ohn	raspberry
hasselnöt _ha_·sehl·nurt	hazelnut
hjortron _yoahr_·tron	cloudberry
jordgubbe _yoard_·guh·ber	strawberry
jordnöt _yoard_·nurt	peanut
katrinplommon ka·_treen_·ploa·mohn	prune
kiwifrukt _kee_·vee·fruhkt	kiwi

kokosnöt _koa_·kos·nurt	coconut
krusbär _kreus_·bair	gooseberry
körsbär _churs_·bair	cherry
lingon lihng·ohn	lingonberry
mandarin man·da·_reen_	tangerine/mandarin orange
mandel _man_·dehl	almond
(vatten)melon (_va_·tehrn)meh·_loan_	(water)melon
mullbär _muhl_·bair	mulberry
nektarin nehk·ta·_reen_	nectarine
oliv o·_leev_	olive
persika _pairsh_·ih·ka	peach
plommon _plohm_·on	plum
pomegranat äpple pom·eh·gra·_naht_·ehp·leh	pomegranate
päron _pai_·rohn	pear
rabarber rah·_bar_·behr	rhubarb
russin _ruh_·sihn	raisin
röd vinbär rurd _veen_·bair	red currant
smultron _smeul_·trohn	wild strawberry
sultana suhl·_tahn_·a	sultana raisin
svart vinbär svart _veen_·bair	black currant
valnöt _vahl_·nurt	walnut
vinbär _veen_·bair	currant
vindruva _veen_·dreu·va	grape
äpple _ehp_·leh	apple

Cheese

fårost _foar_·oast	ewe's milk cheese
getost _yeet_·oast	goat cheese
grevé greh·_vee_	a semi-hard cheese similar to gouda and emmentaler
herrgårdsost _hehr_·goards·oast	a semi-hard cheese with large holes and a nutty flavor

kryddost _krewd•oast_	a sharp, strong cheese with caraway seeds
mesost _mees•oast_	a soft, sweet, yellowish whey cheese
mjukost _myeuk•oast_	soft cheese
ost _oast_	cheese
ostbricka _oast•brih•ka_	cheese plate
prästost _prehst•oast_	hard cheese with a strong, rich flavor
svecia _sveh•see•a_	semi-hard cheeses
västerbotten _vehs•tehr•boh•tehrn_	a sharp, tangy, hard and very strong cheese from the north of Sweden
ädelost _air•dehl•oast_	a blue cheese with a sharp taste, similar to Roquefort

Dessert

efterrätt _ehf•tehr•reht_	dessert
friterad camembert med hjortronsylt _free•tee•rad cam•ehm•behrt meed yoh•tron•sewlt_	deep-fried camembert with cloudberry jam
fruktsallad _fruhkt•sal•ad_	fruit salad
glass _glas_	ice cream
jordgubbar med grädde _yoard•guhb•ar meed greh•deh_	strawberries and cream
kaka _kah•ka_	cake
mandeltårta _man•dehl•toar•ta_	almond tart
marängsviss _mah•rehng•svis_	meringue with whipped cream and chocolate sauce
mjuk pepparkaka _myeuk peh•par•kah•ka_	soft ginger cake
ostkaka _oast•kah•ka_	traditional southern Sweden curd cake

tårta *toarta*	sponge-based fruit or cream cake
våffla (med sylt och grädde) *vohf·la meed sewlt ohk greh·der*	waffle (with jam and whipped cream)
äppelpaj *eh·pehl·pay*	apple tart
äppelkaka *eh·pehl·kah·ka*	apple cake
äppelring *ehp·ehl·rihng*	apple fritter

Sauces & Condiments

peppar *peh·par*	pepper
salt *salt*	salt
senap *see·nap*	mustard
socker *soh·kehr*	sugar
sötningsmedel *surt·nihngs·mee·dehl*	artificial sweetener
ketchup *keht·shuhp*	ketchup

At the Market

Where are the carts [trolleys]/baskets?	**Var finns shoppingvagnarna/shoppingkorgarna?** *vahr fihns shoh·pihng·vagn·nar·na/ shoh·pihng·kohr·yar·na*
Where is/are…?	**Var finns…?** *vahr fihns…*
I'd like some of this/that.	**Jag skulle vilja ha lite av det här/det där.** *yahg skuh·ler vihl·ya hah lee·teh afv dee hair/dee dair*

YOU MAY HEAR…

Kan jag hjälpa er? *kan yahg yehl·pa eer*	Can I help you?
Vad vill ni beställa? *vahd vihl nee beh·steh·la*	What would you like?
Något annat? *noa·goht an·nat*	Anything else?
Det kostar…kronor. *dee kos·tar…kroa·nohr*	That's…kronor.

YOU MAY SEE...

FÖRBRUKAS FÖRE...	best if used by...
KALORIER	calories
FETTFRI	fat free
MÅSTE FÖRVARAS I KYLSKÅP	keep refrigerated
KAN INNEHÅLLA SPÅR AV...	may contain traces of...
BÄST FÖRE...	sell by...
LÄMPLIGT FÖR VEGETARIANER	suitable for vegetarians

Can I taste it?	**Får jag smaka?** *foar yahg smah·ka*
I'd like...	**Jag skulle vilja ha...** *yahg skuh·ler vihl·ya hah...*
a kilo/half-kilo of...	**ett kilo/halvt kilo...** *eht chee·loh/halft chee·loh...*
a liter/half-liter of...	**en liter/halv liter...** *ehn lee·ter/halv lee·ter...*
a piece of...	**en bit av...** *ehn beet afv...*
a slice of...	**en skiva av...** *ehn shee·va afv...*
More/Less than that.	**Mer/Mindre än det där.** *meer/mihn·dreh ehn dee dair*
How much does it cost?	**Hur mycket kostar det?** *heur mew·ker kos·tar dee*
Where do I pay?	**Var kan jag betala?** *vahr kan yahg beh·tah·la*

Measurements in Europe are metric — and that applies to the weight of food too. If you tend to think in pounds and ounces, it's worth brushing up on what the equivalent is before you go shopping for fruit and veg in markets and supermarkets. Fivev hundred grams, or half a kilo, is a common quantity to order, and that converts to just over a pound (17.65 ounces, to be precise).

Although Sweden still has many small, specialty shops, they are slowly giving way to **köpcentrum** (shopping centers), especially in larger towns. You can still find markets that sell fresh fruit and vegetables as well as flowers and some handicrafts. **Julmarknaden** (the traditional Christmas market) in Stockholm is reminiscent of times gone by. Supermarkets can be found in most large towns, cities and suburbs. **Närbutiker** (corner shops), as well as **Pressbyrån** (newsstand chain) sell a good range of food. In Stockholm, **Östermalmshallen** and **Hötorgshallen** (market halls) sell fresh meat — including reindeer and moose — fish and poultry. Swedes enjoy a variety of fish and seafood, and one will find a good selection in most restaurants and supermarkets. If you visit Sweden in August, you will no doubt enjoy a **kräftkalas** (crayfish party). There is not much meat on a crayfish, but when helped down with a few glasses of **akvavit** (aquavit) and some salad and cheese, it makes for an unforgettable evening.

Can I have a bag?	**Kan jag få en påse?** *kan yahg foa ehn poa·seh*
I'm being helped.	**Tack, jag har fått hjälp.** *tak yahg hahr foat yehlp*

For Conversion Tables, see page 185.

In the Kitchen

bottle opener	**flasköppnare** *flask·eup·na·rehr*
bowl	**djup tallrik** *yeup tal·rihk*
can opener	**konservöppnare** *kohn·sehrv·urp·nah·rer*
corkscrew	**korkskruv** *kohrk·skreuv*
cup	**kopp** *kohp*
fork	**gaffel** *gahf·ehl*
frying pan	**stekpanna** *steek·pan·na*
glass	**glas** *glahs*

knife	**kniv** _kneev_	
measuring cup/spoon	**mått/måttsked** _moat/moat·sheed_	
napkin	**servett** _sehr·vehtt_	
plate	**tallrik** _tal·rihk_	
pot	**gryta** _grew·ta_	
saucepan	**kastrull** _kas·truhl_	
spatula	**steekspade** _steek·spah·der_	
spoon	**sked** _sheed_	

Drinks

ESSENTIAL

May I see the wine list/drink menu?	**Kan jag få se vinlistan/drinklistan?** _kan yahg foa see veen·lihs·tan/drihnk·lihs·tan_
What do you recommend?	**Vad rekommenderar ni?** _vahd reh·koh·mehn·dee·rar nee_
I'd like a bottle/glass of red/white wine.	**Jag skulle vilja ha en flaska/ett glas rött/vitt vin.** _yahg skuh·ler vihl·ya hah ehn flas·ka/eht glahs ruhrt/viht veen_
The house wine, please.	**Husets vin, tack.** _heu·sehts veen tak_
Another bottle/glass, please.	**En flaska/Ett glas till, tack.** _ehn flas·ka/eht glahs tihl tak_
I'd like a local beer.	**Jag skulle vilja ha en öl från trakten.** _yahg skuh·ler vihl·ya hah ehn url fron trak·tehn_
Let me buy you a drink.	**Får jag bjuda på en drink.** _foar yahg byeu·da poa ehn drihnk_
Cheers!	**Skål!** _skoal_
A coffee/tea, please.	**En kopp kaffe/te, tack.** _ehn kohp ka·fer/tee tak_

Black.	**Svart.** *Svart*
With…	**Med…** *meed…*
milk	**mjölk** *myuhlk*
sugar	**socker** <u>*soh*</u>*·kehr*
artificial sweetener	**sötningsmedel** <u>*surt*</u>*·nihngs·*<u>*mee*</u>*·dehl*
decaf	**utan koffein** *eu·tan koh·*<u>*feen*</u>
…, please.	**…, tack.** *… tak*
Juice	**Juice** *yoas*
Soda	**sodavatten** *soa·da·va·tehrn*
Sparkling water	**Vatten med kolsyra** <u>*va*</u>*·tehrn meed* <u>*koal*</u>*·*<u>*sew*</u>*·ra*
Still water	**Vatten utan kolsyra** <u>*va*</u>*·tehrn eu·tan* <u>*koal*</u>*·*<u>*sew*</u>*·ra*
Is the tap water safe to drink?	**Kan man dricka kranvattnet?** *kan man* <u>*drih*</u>*·ka* <u>*krahn*</u>*·vat·neht*

Non-alcoholic Drinks

alkoholfri dryck *al·ko·*<u>*hoal*</u>*·free drewk*	non-alcoholic drink
ananasjuice <u>*an*</u>*·a·nas·yoas*	pineapple juice
apelsinjuice *a·pehl·*<u>*seen*</u>*·yoas*	orange juice
cola <u>*koa*</u>*·la*	cola
fruktjuice <u>*fruhkt*</u>*·yoas*	fruit juice
juice *yoas*	juice
kaffe <u>*ka*</u>*·fer*	coffee
läsk *lehsk*	soft drink
milkshake *milk·shake*	milk shake
mineralvatten *mihn·eh·*<u>*rahl*</u>*·va·tehrn*	mineral water
mjölk *myurlk*	milk
saft *saft*	squash (fruit cordial)
sockerdricka <u>*soh*</u>*·kehr·*<u>*drih*</u>*·ka*	lemonade
sodavatten <u>*soa*</u>*·da·va·tehrn*	soda water

YOU MAY HEAR...

Får jag bjuda på en drink? *foar yahg bjeu·da pao ehn drink* — Can I buy you a drink?

Med mjölk/socker? *meed myurlk/soh·ker* — With milk/sugar?

Vatten med/utan kolsyra? *va·tehrn meed/eu·tan koal·sew·ra* — Sparkling/Still water?

thé med mjölk/citron *tee meed myurlk/see·troan* — tea with milk/lemon

tomatjuice *toa·maht·yoas* — tomato juice

tonic *toh·nihk* — tonic water

varmchoklad *varm shoa·klahd* — hot chocolate

vatten med/utan kolsyra *va·tehrn meed/eu·tan koal·sew·ra* — sparkling/still water

For afternoon tea (usually enjoyed with lemon) or coffee you can do no better than the typical Swedish **konditori** (patisserie or coffee shop). Help yourself to as many cups as you like while indulging in a slice of **prinsesstårta** (sponge cake with cream and custard, covered with green marzipan), **mazarin** (almond tart, topped with icing) or a **wienerbröd** (Danish pastry). Try **saffransbullar** (saffron buns) and **pepparkakor** (ginger cookies) at Christmas. Most **konditori** are self-service, but some of the more elegant ones and those in hotels provide full service. Coffee is definitely the national drink, and it is always freshly brewed. It is commonly drunk black, but ask for **mjölk** (milk) or **grädde** (cream) if you like it that way.

Aperitifs, Cocktails & Liqueurs

akvavit *a·kva·veet*	aquavit, the famous Swedish grain- or potato-based spirit
cognac *kohn·yak*	brandy
gin *jihn*	gin
glögg *glurg*	mulled wine with port and spices, served hot
herrgårdsakvavit *hair·goards·a·kva·veet*	aquavit, flavored with caraway seeds and whisky
likör *lih·kurr*	liqueur
portvin *port·veen*	port
punsch *peunsh*	sweet liqueur
rom *rohm*	rum
sherry *sheh·ree*	sherry
skåne *skoa·ner*	aquavit, flavored with aniseed and caraway seeds
sprit *spreet*	spirits
vermouth *vehr·meutt*	vermouth
vodka... *vod·ka...*	vodka...
med is *meed ees*	on the rocks [with ice]
med tonic *meed toh·nihk*	with tonic water

med vatten *meed <u>va</u>·tehrn*	with water
whisky <u>*vihs*</u>·*kee*	whisky

Beer

burköl <u>*buhrk*</u>·*url*	canned beer
fatöl <u>*faht*</u>·*url*	draft [draught]
lättöl <u>*leht*</u>·*url*	light beer
öl på flaska *url poa <u>fla</u>·ska*	bottled beer local/imported
utan alkohol *uh·tan al·koh·hohl*	non-alcoholic

Beer is probably the most popular alcoholic drink in Sweden, and there are many good Swedish breweries. Beer with an alcohol content above 3%, called **starköl**, can only be bought in **Systembolaget** (state liquor store); **lättöl** and **folköl**, which are below 3% alcohol content, can be bought in grocery stores and supermarkets. You will find many well known international beers, but the most common are Carlsberg, Heineken and Swedish brews such as Pripps and Falcon.

Wine

dessertvin *deh·<u>sair</u>·veen*	dessert wine
husets vin <u>*heu*</u>·*sehts veen*	house wine
mousserande *moa·<u>see</u>·ran·der*	sparkling
rosé *roh·<u>seh</u>*	blush [rosé]
rött *ruhrt*	red
sött *suhrt*	sweet
torrt *tohrt*	dry
vitt *viht*	white
champagne *shahm·pany*	champagne

On the Menu

abborre _ah·bohr·er_ — perch

akvavit _a·kva·veet_ — aquavit, the famous Swedish grain- or potato-based spirit

alkoholfri dryck _al·ko·hoal·free drewk_ — non-alcoholic drink

ananas _an·a·nas_ — pineapple

ananasjuice _an·a·nas·yoas_ — pineapple juice

anka _ang·ka_ — duck

ansjovis _an·shoa·vees_ — anchovy

apelsin _a·pehl·seen_ — orange

apelsinjuice _a·pehl·seen·yoas_ — orange juice

aprikos _a·prih·koas_ — apricot

avokado _a·voh·kah·doa_ — avocado

bacon _bay·kon_ — bacon

bakelse _bah·kehl·sehr_ — piece of cake

bakverk _bahk·verk_ — pastry

banan _ba·nahn_ — banana

basilika _ba·sih·lee·ka_ — basil

biffkött _bihf·churt_ — beef

biffstek _bif·steek_ — steak

bigarrå *bih·ga·roa*	sweet morello cherry
bit *beet*	slice
björnbär *byurn·bair*	blackberry
blandade *blan·da·der*	assorted
blandade grönsaker *blan·da·der grurn·sah·kehr*	mixed vegetables
blandade kryddor *blan·da·der krew·dohr*	mixed herbs
blandade nötter *blan·da·der nur·tehr*	assorted nuts
blandsallad *bland·sal·ad*	mixed salad
blodig *bloa·dihg*	rare
blomkål *bloam·koal*	cauliflower
blå vindruva *bloa veen·dreu·va*	black grape
blåbär *bloa·bair*	blueberry
blåbärssylt *bloa·bairs·sewlt*	blueberry jam
blåmussla *bloa·muhs·la*	blue mussel
bog *boag*	shoulder (cut of meat)
bondböna *boand·bur·nohr*	broad bean
bordsvin *boards·veen*	table wine
bouquet garni *boh·keh gar·nee*	mixed herbs
braxen *brak·sehn*	sea bream
broccoli *broh·loh·lee*	broccoli

broiler _broy_·lehr	spring chicken
brylépudding brew·_lee_·peu·dihng	crème brulee
brysselkål _brew_·sehl·koal	brussel sprout
brytböna _brewt_·bur·na	kidney bean
brännvin _brehn_·veen	aquavit, grain or potato based spirit
bröd brurd	bread
brödsmulor _brurd_·smeu·lohr	bread crumbs
bröst brurst	breast
buljong buhl·_yong_	broth
bulle _buh_·ler	bun
burköl _buhrk_·url	canned beer
bål boal	punch
böckling _burk_·lihng	smoked herring
böna _bur_·na	bean [pulses]
bönskott _burn_·skoht	bean sprout
champinjon sham·pihn·_yoan_	mushroom
chilipeppar _shee_·lih·_peh_·par	chili pepper
chips shihps	potato chips [crisps]
choklad shoa·_klahd_	chocolate
citron see·_troan_	lemon
citronjuice see·_troan_·yoas	lemon juice
cognac _kohn_·yak	brandy
cola _koa_·la	cola
dadel _dahd_·ehl	date
dagens meny _dah_·gehns meh·_neu_	menu of the day
dagens rätt _dah_·gehns rairtt	speciality of the day
dessertvin deh·_sair_·veen	dessert wine
dillsås _dihl_·soas	dill sauce
dragon dra·_goan_	tarragon
dryck med alkohol drewk meed _al_·ko·hoal	alcoholic drink

efterrätt _ehf·tehr·rairt_	dessert
en halv flaska _ehn halv fla·ska_	half bottle
enbär _een·bair_	juniper berry
endiv _an·deev_	endive
entrecote _an·treh·koa_	sirloin steak
falukorv _fah·leu·kohrv_	lightly spiced sausage
fasan _fa·sahn_	pheasant
fatöl _faht·url_	draft [draught] beer
fikon _fee·kohn_	fig
filé _fih·leh_	filet mignon
filmjölk _feel·mjurlk_	thick yogurt
fisk _fihsk_	fish
fisk och skaldjur _fihsk·ohk·skahl·yeur_	fish and seafood
fisksoppa _fihsk·sop·a_	fish soup
fläsk _flehsk_	pork
fläskben _flehsk·been_	ham bone
fläskfilé _flehsk·fih·leh_	fillet of pork
fläskkarré _flehsk·ka·reh_	pork loin
fläskkorv _flehsk·kohrv_	spicy, boiled pork sausage
fläsklägg _flehsk·lehg_	knuckle of pork
fläskpannkaka _flehsk·pan·kah·ka_	thick pancake filled with bacon
forell _foa·rehl_	trout
franskbröd _fransk·brurd_	French bread
friterad camembert med hjortronsylt _free·tee·rad cam·ehm·behrt meed yoh·tron·sewlt_	deep-fried Camembert with cloudberry jam
frukost _fruh·kohst_	breakfast
frukostflingor _fruhkost·flihng·ohr_	(cold) cereal
frukt _fruhkt_	fruit
fruktjuice _fruhkt·yoas_	fruit juice
fruktsallad _fruhkt·sal·ad_	fruit salad

fullkornsmjöl _fuhl_·kohrns·my**url**	whole wheat flour
fylld (med) fewld (meed)	stuffed (with)
fylld oliv _fewld_ o·_leev_	stuffed olive
fylligt _few_·liht	full-bodied (wine)
fågel _foa_·gehl	poultry
får foar	mutton
fårost _foar_·oast	ewe's milk cheese
fänkål _fehn_·koal	fennel
färsk (frukt) fehrsk (fruhkt)	fresh (fruit)
färsk fikon fairsk _fee_·kohn	fresh fig
färska räkor _fairs_·ka _rair_·kohr	unshelled shrimp [prawns]
färskpotatis _fairsk_·poa·_tah_·tihs	new potato
förlorat ägg furr·_loa_·rat ehg	poached egg
förrätt _furr_·rairt	appetizer [starter]
garnering gar·_nee_·rihng	garnish
gelé sheh·_leh_	jelly
get yeet	kid (goat)
getost _yeet_·oast	goat cheese
gin jihn	gin
glass glas	ice cream
glutenfritt _glue_·tehn·friht	gluten free

glögg _glurg_ — mulled wine with port and spices, served hot

grapefrukt _grahp_·fruhkt — grapefruit
gratinerad gra·tih·_nee_·rad — au gratin
gratäng gra·_tehng_ — casserole
gravlax _grafv_·lax — marinated salmon
grevé greh·_veh_ — semi-hard cheese
grillad kyckling _grihl_·ahd _chewk_·lihng — grilled chicken
grillspett _grihl_·speht — skewer
gryta _grew_·ta — pot roast, stew or casserole
grädde _greh_·der — cream
gräddfil _grehd_·feel — sour cream
gräslök _grairs_·**lurk** — chive
grön böna _grur_·na _bur_·na — green bean
grön paprika grurn _pah_·pree·ka — green pepper
grön vindruva _grurn_ veen·d**reu**·va — green grape
grönsak _grurn_·sahk — vegetable
grönsakssoppa _grurn_·sahks·_sohp_·a — vegetable soup
grönsallad _grurn_·sal·ad — green salad
gröt _grurt_ — (hot) cereal
gurka _geur_·ka — cucumber
gås _goas_ — goose
gädda _yeh_·da — sea perch
hallon _hal_·ohn — raspberry
halstrad fisk _hal_·strahd fihsk — grilled fish
halstrad forell med färskpotatis _hal_·strad foa·_rehl_ med fairsk·poa·_tah_·this — grilled trout with new potatoes
hamburgare _ham_·beur·ya·rer — hamburger
hare _hah_·rer — rabbit
haricots verts ar·ee·koh·_vair_ — string beans

hasselbackspotatis	oven-baked potato, coated
ha·sehl·baks·poa·tah·tihs	in bread crumbs
hasselnöt _ha·sehl·nurt_	hazelnut
havre _hafv·rer_	oats
havregryn _hafv·reh·greun_	oatmeal
havsabborre _hafs·a·boh·rer_	sea bass
hemlagad _hehm·lah·gad_	homemade
herrgårdsakvavit	aquavit flavored with
hair·goards·a·kva·veet	caraway seeds and whisky
herrgårdsost _hehr·goards·oast_	semi-hard cheese with
	a nutty flavor
hett _heht_	hot (temperature)
hjort _yohrt_	deer
hjortron _yoahr·tron_	cloudberry
hjortron sylt _yoar·trohn·sewlt_	cloudberry jam
honung _hoa·neung_	honey
hovmästarsås _hoav·mehs·tar·soas_	dill sauce
hummer _huhm·ehr_	lobster
husets specialitet _heu·sehts speh·sih·al·ee·teet_	specialty of the house
husets vin _heu·sehts veen_	house wine
huvudrätt _heu·vuhd·rait_	main course

hårdkokt ägg _hoard_·kohkt ehg	hard-boiled egg
hårt bröd _hoart brurd_	crispbread
hälleflundra _heh·leh·fleun·dra_	halibut
ingefära _ih·ng·eh·fai·ra_	ginger
inlagd i ättika (vinäger) _ihn·lahgd ee eh·tih·ka_	marinated in vinegar
inlagd sill _ihn·lahgd sil_	marinated (pickled) herring
is _ees_	ice
isterband _ihs·tehr·band_	sausage of pork, barley and beef
Janssons frestelse _yahn·sons frehs·tehl·ser_	casserole with potatoes and anchovies
jordgubbar med grädde _yoard·guhb·ar meed greh·deh_	strawberries and cream
jordgubbe _yoard·guh·ber_	strawberry
jordnöt _yoard·nurt_	peanut
juice _yoas_	juice
julbord _yeul·board_	buffet of hot and cold Swedish specialties served at Christmas time
kaffe _ka·fer_	coffee

kaka _kah·ka_	cake
kalkon _kal·koan_	turkey
kall soppa _kal sohp·a_	cold soup
kallskuret _kal·skeu·reht_	cold cuts
kalops _ka·lohps_	beef stew
kalvbräss _kalv·brehs_	sweetbread
kalvkött _kalv·churt_	veal
kalvsylta _kalv·sewl·ta_	cold veal in jelly
kammussla _kam·muhs·la_	scallop
kanderad frukt _kan·deeh·rahd fruhkt_	candied fruit
kanel _ka·neel_	cinnamon
kantarell _kan·ta·rehl_	chanterelle mushroom
kapris _ka·prees_	caper
karaff _ka·raff_	carafe
karameller _ka·ra·mehl·ehr_	candy [sweets]
karré _ka·reh_	tenderloin
katrinplommon _ka·treen·ploa·mohn_	prune
kex _kehx_	cookie [biscuit]
kikärta _cheek·air·ta_	chickpea
kiwifrukt _kee·vee·fruhkt_	kiwi
klimp _klihmp_	dumpling
kokosnöt _koa·kos·nurt_	coconut
kokt katrinplommon _koakt ka·treen·ploa·mohn_	stewed prune
kokt potatis _koakt poa·tah·tihs_	boiled potato
kokt skinka _koakt shihng·ka_	boiled ham
kokt ägg _koakt ehg_	boiled egg
kolja _kohl·ya_	haddock
kolsyrad _koal·sew·rad_	carbonated
kompott _kom·poht_	stewed fruit
konserverad frukt _kon·ser·vee·rad fruhkt_	canned fruit

korv *kohrv*	sausage
kotlett *koht·lehtt*	cutlet
krabba *kra·ba*	crab
kronärtskocka *kroan·airts·koh·ka*	artichoke
kroppkaka *kropp·kah·ka*	potato dumpling, filled with bacon and onions
krusbär *kreus·bair*	gooseberry
krydda *krew·da*	spice
kryddad *krew·dad*	spicy
kryddad pepparsås *krew·dahd peh·par·soas*	hot pepper sauce
kryddost *krewd·oast*	sharp, strong cheese with caraway seeds
kryddpeppar *krewd·peh·par*	allspice
kryddstarkt *krewd·starkt*	spicy
kräfta *krehf·ta*	crayfish
kummel *keu·mel*	hake
kummin *keu·meen*	caraway
kvark *kvark*	fresh curd cheese
kyckling *chewk·lihng*	chicken
kycklingbröst *chewk·lihng·brurst*	chicken breast
kycklinglever *chewk·lihng·lee·vehr*	chicken liver
kycklingsoppa *chewk·lihng·sohp·a*	chicken soup
kyld dryck *chewl drewk*	cold drink
kylt *chewlt*	chilled (wine, etc.)
kål *koal*	cabbage
kåldolmar *koal·dohl·mar*	cabbage leaves stuffed with chopped [minced] meat and rice
kålrot *koal·roht*	turnip
källkrasse *chehl·kra·se*	watercress
körsbär *churs·bair*	cherry

körvel _chur_•vehl	chervil
kött _churt_	meat
kött och grönsakssoppa	meat and vegetable
churt•oa•_grurn_•sahk•_sohp_•a	soup
köttbulle _churt_•buh•ler	meatball
köttfärs _churt_•fairs	chopped [minced] beef
köttsoppa _churt_•sohp•a	beef and vegetable soup
	with dumplings
köttsås _churt_•s_oa_s	meat sauce
lagerblad _lah_•gehr•blahd	bay leaf
lageröl _lah_•ger•**url**	lager
lamm _lamm_	lamb
lammgryta _lamm_•gr**ew**•ta	lamb stew
landgång _land_•goang	long open-faced sandwich
lax _lax_	salmon
lever _lee_•vehr	liver
leverpastej _lee_•vehr pa•_stay_	liver pâté
lingon _lihng_•ohn	lingonberry
lingonsylt _lihng_•ohn•sewlt	lingonberry jam
lins _lihns_	lentil
likör _lih_•**kurr**	liqueur

lägg *lehg*	shank (top of leg)
läsk *lehsk*	soft drink
lättöl *leht·ur*	light beer
löjrom *lury·rohm*	bleak roe with chopped, raw onions and sour cream; served on toast
lök *lurk*	onion
löksoppa *lurk·sohp·a*	onion soup
lövbiff *lurv·bihf*	fried, thinly sliced beef, with onions
majonnäs *may·oha·nairs*	mayonnaise
majs *mays*	sweet corn
makrill *mahk·rihl*	mackerel
mandarin *man·da·reen*	tangerine/mandarin orange
mandel *man·dehl*	almond
mandeltårta *man·dehl·toar·ta*	almond tart
marmelad *mahr·meh·lahd*	marmalade
marsipan *mahr·sih·pahn*	marzipan
marulk *mahr·eulk*	monkfish
maräng *mah·rehng*	meringue
marängsviss *mah·rehng·svihs*	meringue served with cream and chocolate sauce

matjesill _ma_·shcheh·sihl	marinated herring
med citron _meed_ see·_troan_	with lemon
med florsocker _meed_ _floar_·soh·ker	with icing
med grädde _meed_ _greh_·der	with cream
med is _meed_ ees	with ice
med kolsyra _meed_ _koal_·_sew_·ra	carbonated (drink)
med mjölk _meed_ my_urlk_	with milk
med socker _meed_ _soh_·kehr	with sugar
med tonic _meed_ _toh_·nihk	with tonic water
med vatten _meed_ _va_·tehrn	with water
med vitlök _meed_ _veet_·l_urk_	with garlic
medaljong meh·dal·yong	small fillet of cut meat
medium _meh_·_dee_·yuhm	medium
mellanmål meh·lan·_moal_	snack
(vatten)melon (_va_·tehrn)meh·_loan_	(water)melon
meny meh·_neu_	menu
mesost _mees_·oast	soft, sweet whey cheese
middag _mih_·dahg	dinner
milkshake _milk_·shake	milk shake
mineralvatten mih·neh·_rahl_·va·tehrn	mineral water
mjuk pepparkaka my_euk_ _peh_·par·kah·ka	soft ginger cake
mjukost _myeuk_·oast	soft cheese
mjöl my_url_	flour
mjölk my_urlk_	milk
mogen _moa_·gehn	ripe
morot _moa_·roht	carrot
mousserande moa·_see_·ran·der	sparkling (wine)
muffin _muh_·fihn	muffin
mullbär _muhl_·b_air_	mulberry
multe _muhl_·ter	mullet
munk _muhnk_	donut

muskot _muhs_•koht	nutmeg
müsli _mews_•lee	granola [muesli]
mussla _muhs_•la	mussel
mustigt _muhs_•tihkt	full-bodied (wine)
mycket kryddad _mew_•keht _krew_•dad	highly seasoned
mycket torrt _mew_•keht tohrt	very dry (wine, etc.)
mynta _mewn_•ta	mint (herb)
mäktig _mehk_•tihg	rich (sauce)
mördegstårta _muhr_•deegs•_toar_•ta	tart (sweet or savory)
mört murtt	roach (type of fish)
nejlika _nay_•lih•ka	clove
nektarin nehk•ta•_reen_	nectarine
njure _nyeu_•rer	kidney
nudel _neu_•dehl	noodle
nyponsoppa _new_•pohn•sohp•a	rose-hip soup
nötkött _nurt_•churt	red meat
odlade champinjon _oad_•lah•der	cultivated mushroom
sham•peen•_yoa_n	
ojäst bröd oa•_yairst_ brurd	unleavened bread
oliv o•_leev_	olive
olja och vinäger _oal_•ya ohk vee•_nai_•gehr	oil and vinegar
omelett om•eh•_leht_	omelet
ost oast	cheese
ostbricka _oast_•brih•ka	cheese plate
ostkaka _oast_•kah•ka	curd cake served with jam
ostkex _oast_•kehx	cheese cracker
ostron _oa_•strohn	oyster
oxkött _oax_•churt	ox
oxrullad _oax_•reu•_lahd_	braised roll of beef
oxsvans _oax_•svans	oxtail
oxsvanssoppa _oax_•svans•_sohp_•a	oxtail soup

paj *pay*	pie
palsternacka *pal·stehr·na·ka*	parsnip
pannbiff *pan·bihf*	beef patty
pannkaka *pan·kah·ka*	pancake
paprika *pah·prih·ka*	pepper (fresh)
pasta *pas·ta*	pasta
pastarätt *pas·ta·rairt*	pasta dish
pastej *pa·stay*	pâté
peppar *peh·par*	pepper (condiment)
pepparkaka *peh·par·kah·ka*	ginger cookie
pepparrotssås *peh·pa·roat·soas*	horseradish sauce
persika *pair·shih·ka*	peach
persilja *pair·shihl·ya*	parsley
piggvar *pihg·vahr*	turbot
pitabröd *pee·ta·brurd*	pita bread
plommon *ploa·mohn*	plum
plättar *pleh·tar*	small pancakes served with jam and whipped cream
pomegranat äpple *pom·eh·gra·naht·ehp·leh*	pomegranate
pommes frites *pohm·friht*	French fries
portion *pohrt·shoan*	portion

portvin _pohrt_·veen	port
potatis poa·_tah_·tihs	potato
potatismos poa·_tah_·tihs·moas	mashed potatoes
potatissoppa poa·_tah_·tihs·_sohp_·a	potato soup
prinsesstårta prihn·_sehs_·to**ar**·ta	sponge cake with (vanilla) custard, whipped cream and jam, covered in light green marzipan
prinskorv _prihns_·kohrv	small pork sausage
prästost _prehst_·oast	hard cheese with a strong, rich flavor
pumpa _puhm_·pa	pumpkin
punsch peunsh	sweet liqueur
purjolök _peur_·yoh·**lur**k	leek
pytt i panna _pewt_·ee·pa·na	chunks of fried meat, onion and potatoes
på beställning poa beh·_stehl_·nihng	made on request
pärlande _pair_·lan·der	sparkling
pärlhöns _pairl_·hurns	guinea fowl
päron _pai_·rohn	pear
rabarber rah·_bar_·behr	rhubarb

ragu *ra·gue*	beef stew
rapphöna *rap·hurna*	partridge
ren *reen*	reindeer
renat *ree·nat*	flavorless, clear spirit (aquavit)
renstek *reen·steek*	roast reindeer
revbensspjäll *reev·beens·spehl*	spareribs
riktigt blodig *rihk·tihgt bloa·dihg*	very rare
rimmad lax *rih·mad lax*	lightly salted salmon
ris *rees*	rice
rocka *roh·ka*	ray (type of fish)
rom *rohm*	rum
rosé *roh·seh*	blush (wine)
rosmarin *roas·ma·reen*	rosemary
rostat bröd *rohs·tat brurd*	toast
rostbiff *rohst·bihf*	roast beef
rova *roa·va*	turnip
rumpstek *ruhmp·steek*	rump steak
russin *ruh·sihn*	raisin
rå *roa*	raw
rådjur *roa·yeur*	venison
rådjursstek *roa·yeur·steek*	roast of venison
rågbröd *roag·brurd*	rye bread
rädisa *raid·dih·sa*	radish
räkor *rair·kohr*	shrimp [prawns]
rätt *reht*	dish
röd paprika *rurd pah·pree·ka*	sweet red pepper
röd vinbär *rurd veen·bair*	red currant
rödbeta *rurd·bee·ta*	beet
röding *rur·dihng*	char
rödkål *rurd·koal*	red cabbage

rödspätta <u>rurd</u>·speh·ta	plaice
rökt fisk rurkt fisk	smoked fish
rökt lax rurkt lax	smoked salmon
rökt renstek rurkt <u>reen</u>·steek	smoked reindeer
rökt skinka rurkt <u>shihng</u>·ka	smoked ham
rökt ål rurkt oal	smoked eel
rörd soppa rurrd <u>sohp</u>·a	cream soup
rött rurt	red (wine)
sadel <u>sah</u>·dehl	saddle (cut of meat)
saffransbullar <u>sa</u>·frans·buh·lar	Christmas saffron buns
saft saft	squash (fruit cordial)
salamikorv sa·lah·<u>mee</u>·kohrv	salami
sallad <u>sal</u>·ad	salad
salladshuvud <u>sal</u>·ads·heu·vuhd	head of lettuce
salt salt	salt
saltade jordnötter <u>sal</u>·ta·der <u>yoard</u>·nur·ter	salted peanuts
saltgurka <u>salt</u>·geur·ka	salted, pickled gherkin
salvia sal·<u>vee</u>·a	sage
sardin sar·<u>deen</u>	sardine
schalottenlök sha·loh·<u>tehn</u>·lurk	shallot
schnitzel <u>shniht</u>·sehl	escallope
selleri seh·leh·<u>ree</u>	celery
senap <u>see</u>·nap	mustard
sherry sheh·<u>ree</u>	sherry
sill sihl	herring
sillbricka <u>sihl</u>·brih·ka	variety of marinated herring
sillsallad <u>sihl</u>·sal·ad	beet and herring salad
sirap <u>seh</u>·rap	syrup
sjömansbiff <u>shur</u>·mans·bihf	casserole of fried beef, onions and potatoes, braised in beer
sjötunga <u>sjur</u>·teung·a	sole

skaldjur _skahl·y**eur**_	shellfish
skaldjurssallad _skahl·yeurs·sal·ad_	shellfish salad
skarpsill _skarp·sihl_	herring
skinka _skihng·ka_	ham
skogssvamp _skoags·svamp_	field mushroom
sky _shewy_	gravy
skåne _sk**oa**·ner_	type of aquavit flavored with aniseed and caraway
smultron _smeul·trohn_	wild strawberry
småbröd _sm**oa**·brurd_	roll
småkaka _sm**oa**·kah·ka_	cookie [biscuit]
smårätt _sm**oa**·rairt_	snack
småsill _sm**oa**·sihl_	herring
smör _smur_	butter
smördeg _smur·deeg_	pastry
smörgås _smur·g**oa**s_	Swedish open-faced sandwich
snigel _sneeg·ehl_	snail
socker _soh·kehr_	sugar
sockerdricka _soh·kehr·drih·ka_	lemonade
sockerkaka _soh·kehr·kah·ka_	sponge cake

sockerärta _soh·kehr·air·ta_ — sugar snap pea [mangetout]

sodavatten _soa·da·va·tehrn_ — soda water

soppa _sohp·a_ — soup

S.O.S. (smör, ost och sill) _ehs oa ehs_
(smur oast ohk sihl) — small plate of marinated herring, read, butter and cheese

sparris _spar·ihs_ — asparagus

sparrissoppa _spa·rihs·sohp·a_ — asparagus soup

specialitet för landsdelen — local specialty
speh·sih·ahl·ih·teet furr lands·deel·ehn

spenat _speh·naht_ — spinach

spenatsoppa _speh·naht·sohp·a_ — spinach soup

sprit _spreet_ — spirits

spädgris _spaird·grees_ — unweaned piglet

squash _skoawsh_ — squash (vegetable)

stark _stark_ — strong (flavor)

starkt kryddad _starkt krew·dad_ — hot (spicy)

stek _steek_ — roast

stekt fisk _steekt fisk_ — fried fish

stekt kyckling _steekt chewk·lihng_ — fried chicken (not breaded)

stekt potatis _steekt poa·tah·tihs_ — sautéed potato

stekt ägg _steekt ehg_ — fried egg

strömming _strurm·ihng_ — sprats (small Baltic herring)

strömmingsflundra
strurm·ihngs·fleun·dra — Baltic herring, filleted and sandwiched in pairs, fried, with dill and butter filling

stuvad abborre _steu·vad a·bohr·er_ — perch poached with onion, parsley and lemon

sufflé _suh·fleh_ — soufflé

sultana _suhl·tahn·a_ — sultana raisin

sur _seur_ — sour

svamp *svamp*	mushroom
svart vinbär <u>*svart*</u> *veen·bair*	black currant
svecia <u>*sveh*</u>*·see·a*	semi-hard cheese
svensk punsch <u>*sven*</u>*·sk peunsh*	Swedish punch (sweet liqueur)
sylt *sewlt*	jam
sås *soas*	sauce
sötningsmedel <u>*surt*</u>*·nihngs·*<u>*mee*</u>*·dehl*	artificial sweetener
sötpotatis *surt·poa·*<u>*tah*</u>*·tihs*	sweet potato
sötsur sås <u>*surt*</u>*·seur soas*	sweet-and-sour sauce
sött *suht*	sweet
T-benstek <u>*tee*</u>*·been·steek*	T-bone steak
thé *tee*	tea
timjan *tihm·*<u>*yan*</u>	thyme
toast skagen *toast* <u>*skah*</u>*·gehn*	toast with chopped shrimp in mayonnaise, topped with bleak roe
tomat *toa·*<u>*maht*</u>	tomato
tomater och lök *toa·*<u>*mah*</u>*·ter ohk* **l**u**rk**	tomato and onion salad
tomatjuice *toa·*<u>*maht*</u>*·yoas*	tomato juice
tomatsoppa *toa·*<u>*maht*</u>*·soh·pa*	tomato soup

tomatsås *toa·maht·soas*	tomato sauce
tonfisk *toan·fihsk*	tuna
tonic *toh·nihk*	tonic water
torkade dadel *tohr·ka·der dah·dehl*	dried date
torkade fikon *tohr·ka·der fee·kohn*	dried fig
torrt *tohrt*	dry
torsk *torshk*	cod
tunga *tuhng·a*	tongue (cow)
tunn sås *tuhnn soas*	light (sauce)
tunnbröd *tuhnn·brurd*	Swedish flat bread, can be soft or crispy
tårta *toarta*	sponge-based fruit or cream cake
ugnsbakad fisk *eungns·bah·kad fihsk*	oven-baked fish
ugnsstekt kyckling *eungn·steekt chewk·lihng*	roast chicken
ugnsstekt potatis *eungn·steekt poa·tah·tihs*	roast potato
utan koffein *eu·tan ko·feen*	decaffeinated
vaktel *vak·tehl*	quail
valfria tillbehör *vahl·free·a tihl·beh·hurr*	choice of side dishes
valnöt *vahl·nurt*	walnut

vanilj _va·nihly_	vanilla
vaniljsås _va·nihly·soas_	vanilla sauce, often like custard
varmchoklad _varm shoa·klahd_	hot chocolate
varmkorv _varm kohrv_	hot dog
varmrätt _varm·rairt_	warm meal, usually main course
varmt _varmt_	hot
vatten _va·tehrn_	water
vattenkrasse _va·tehrn·kra·ser_	watercress
vaxböna _vax·bur·na_	butter bean
vegetarisk meny _vehg·eh·tah·risk meh·neu_	vegetarian menu
vermouth _vehr·meutt_	vermouth
vetemjöl _vee·teh·mjurl_	wheat flour (regular)
whisky _vihs·kee_	whisky
wienerbröd _vee·nehr·brurd_	Danish pastry
wienerschnitzel _vee·nehr·shniht·sehl_	breaded veal cutlet
vild champinjon _vihl·da sham·pihn·yoan_	wild mushroom
vildand _vihld·and_	wild duck
vilt _vihlt_	game
viltpastej _vihlt·pa·stay_	game pâté
vin _veen_	wine
vinaigrettesås _vih·neh·greht·soas_	vinaigrette [French dressing]
vinbär _veen·bair_	currant
vindruva _veen·dreu·va_	grape
vinlista _veen·lihs·ta_	wine list
vispgrädde _visp·greh·der_	whipped cream
vit sås _veet soas_	white sauce
vitkål _veet·koal_	white cabbage
vitkålssallad _veet·koal·sal·ad_	coleslaw
vitling _veet·lihng_	whiting

vitlök _veet·lurk_	garlic
vitlöksmajonnäs _veet·lurks·may·oa·nairs_	garlic mayonnaise
vitlökssås _veet·lurk·soas_	garlic sauce
vinbär _veen·bair_	currant
vindruva _veen·dreu·va_	grape
vinlista _veen·lihs·ta_	wine list
vispgrädde _visp·greh·der_	whipped cream
vitt _viht_	white (wine)
vitt bröd _viht brurd_	white bread
vodka _vod·ka_	vodka
vol au vent _vohl·oa·vahnt_	vol-au-vent (pastry filled with meat or fish)
våffla (med sylt och grädde) _vohf·la meed sewlt ohk greh·der_	waffle (with jam and whipped cream)
vårlök _voar lurk_	shallot [spring onion]
västerbotten _vehs·tehr·boh·tehn_	strong, tangy, hard cheese
västkustsallad _vehst·kuhst·sal·ad_	west coast salad, with shrimp [prawns] and mussels
yoghurt _yoa·geurt_	yogurt
zucchini _seu·kee·nee_	zucchini [courgette]
ål _oal_	eel

ångkokt fisk _oang_·koakt fisk	steamed fish
ädelost _air_·dehl·oast	blue cheese
ägg _ehg_	egg
äggplanta _ehg_·plan·ta	eggplant [aubergine]
äggula _ehg_·geu·la	egg yolk
äggröra _ehg_·rur·ra	scrambled egg
äggvita _ehg_·vee·ta	egg white
älg _ehly_	moose
älgfilé _ehly_·fih·_leh_	fillet of moose
älgstek _ehly_·steek	moose roast
älgstek med svampsås _ehly_·steek meed _svamp_·**so**as	roast moose with mushroom sauce
äppelkaka _eh_·pehl·_kah_·ka	apple cake
äppelpaj _ehp_·ehl·_pay_	apple tart
äppelring _ehp_·ehl·rihng	apple fritter
äpple _ehp_·leh	apple
ärta _air_·ta	pea
ärtsoppa _airt_·sohp·a	green or yellow pea soup
ättiksgurka _eh_·tihks·geur·ka	sweet, pickled gherkins
öl _url_	beer
öl på flaska _url_ poa _fla_·ska	bottled beer

People

ESSENTIAL

Hello!	**Hej!** *hay*
How are you?	**Hur står det till?** *heur stoar dee tihl*
Fine, thanks. And you?	**Bra, tack. Och du?** *brah tak ohk deu*
Excuse me!	**Ursäkta!** *eur·shehk·ta*
Do you speak English?	**Talar du engelska?** *tah·lar deu ehng·ehl·ska*
What's your name?	**Vad heter du?** *vahd hee·tehr deu*
My name is…	**Jag heter…** *yahg hee·tehr…*
Nice to meet you.	**Trevligt att träffas.** *treev·lihgt at trehf·as.*
Where are you from?	**Var kommer du ifrån?** *vahr ko·mehr deu ee·froan*
I'm from the	**Jag kommer från USA/Storbritannien.**
U.S./U.K.	*yahg koh·mehr froan eu ehs ah/stoap·bree·tan·yehn*
What do you do?	**Vad sysslar du med?** *vahd sews·lar deu meed*
I work for…	**Jag jobbar på.** *yahg yohb·ar poa…*
I'm a student.	**Jag är student.** *yahg air stuh·dent*
I'm retired.	**Jag är pensionär.** *yahg air pang·shoa·nair*
Do you like…?	**Tycker du om…?** *tew·kehr deu ohm…*
Goodbye.	**Hej då.** *hay·doa*
See you later.	**Vi ses.** *vee sees*

Language Difficulties

Do you speak English?	**Talar du engelska?**	_tah_·lar deu _ehng_·ehl·ska
Does anyone here speak English?	**Talar någon engelska här?**	_tah_·lar _noa_·gohn _ehng_·ehl·ska hair
I don't speak Swedish.	**Jag talar inte svenska.**	yahg _tah_·lar ihn·ter _svehn_·ska
Could you speak more slowly?	**Kan du tala lite långsammare?**	kan deu _tah_·la _lee_·ter _loang_·sam·a·rer
Could you repeat that?	**Kan du upprepa det?**	kan deu _uhp_·ree·pah d_ee_
Excuse me?	**Ursäkta?**	_eur_·shehk·ta
What was that?	**Vad var det?**	vahd vahr d_ee_
Can you spell it?	**Kan du stava det?**	kahn deu _stah_·va deht
Write it down, please.	**Skriv ner det, tack.**	skreev neer dee tak
Can you translate this for me?	**Kan du översätta det här?**	kan deu _ur_·ver·seh·ta deet hair
What does this/that mean?	**Vad betyder det här/där?**	vad beh·_tew_·der d_ee_ hair/dair
I understand.	**Jag förstår.**	yahg furr·_stoar_
I don't understand.	**Jag förstår inte.**	yahg furr·_stoar_ ihn·ter
Do you understand?	**Förstår du?**	furr·_stoar_ deu

YOU MAY HEAR...

Jag talar bara lite engelska. yahg _tah_·lar _bah_·ra _lee_·ter _ehng_·ehl·ska

I speak only a little English.

Jag talar inte engelska. yahg _tah_·lar _in_·ter _ehng_·ehl·ska

I don't speak English.

Swedes shake hands when greeting someone and when saying goodbye; this applies for meeting new people but is also often the case with colleagues or acquaintances. When you meet someone for the first time, shake hands and give your name. As in many countries, titles are more commonly used by the older generation, but you will sometimes hear **herr** (Mr.), **fru** (Mrs.) and **fröken** (Miss) used, as well as professional titles, e.g., **doktor** (doctor), **ingenjör** (engineer), etc.

Making Friends

Hello.	**Hej.** *hay*
Good morning.	**God morgon.** *goad mor·on*
Good afternoon.	**God middag.** *goad mi·dahg*
Good evening.	**God afton.** *goad af·tohn*
My name is...	**Jag heter...** *yahg hee·tehr...*
What's your name?	**Vad heter du?** *vahd hee·tehr deu*
I'd like to introduce you to...	**Får jag presentera...** *foar yahg preh·sehn·tee·ra...*
Pleased to meet you.	**Trevligt att träffas.** *treev·lihgt at treh·fas*

How are you?	**Hur står det till?** *heur stoar dee tihl*
Fine, thanks.	**Bra, tack.** *brah tak*
And you?	**Och du?** *ohk deu*

Travel Talk

I'm here...	**Jag är här...** *yahg air hair...*
on business	**på affärsresa** *poa a-fairs-ree-sa*
on vacation [holiday]	**på semester** *poa seh-mehs-tehr*
studying	**för studier** *furr steu-de-ehr*
I'm staying for...	**Jag ska stanna i...** *yahg skah sta-na ee...*
I've been here..	**Jag har varit här i...** *yahg hahr vah-riht hair ee...*
a day	**en dag** *ehn dahg*
a week	**en vecka** *ehn veh-ka*
a month	**en månad** *ehn moa-nad*
Where are you from?	**Var kommer du ifrån?** *vahr koh-mehr deu ee-froan*
I'm from.	**Jag kommer från.** *yahg koh-mehr froan...*

For Numbers, see page 179.

Personal

Who are you here with?	**Vem är du här med?** *vehm air deu hair meed*
I'm on my own.	**Jag är ensam.** *yahg air ehn-sam*
I'm with...	**Jag är här med...** *yahg air hair meed...*
my husband/wife	**min man/fru** *mihn man/freu*
my boyfriend	**min pojkvän** *mihn povk-vehn*
girlfriend	**flickvän** *flihk-vehn*
a friend/friends	**en vän/vänner** *ehn vehn/venhn-ehr*
a colleague colleagues	**en kollega** *ehn koh-lee-ga/* **kolleger** *koh-lee-goahr*
When's your birthday?	**När fyller du år?** *nair fewl-ehr deu oar*

How old are you?	**Hur gammal är du?** heur _gah_·mal air deu
I'm...	**Jag är...** yahg air...
single	**ogift** _oa_·yift
in a relationship	**i ett förhållande** ee eht furr·_hoal_·an·der
engaged	**förlovad** fuhr·loh·vad
married	**gift** yihft
divorced	**skild** shihld
separated	**separerad** seh·pa·_ree_·rad
I'm a widow/widower.	**Jag är änka/änkling.** yahg air _ehng_·ka/_ehnak_·lihna
Do you have children/ grandchildren?	**Har du barn/barnbarn?** hahr deu bahrn/_bahrn_·bahrn

For Numbers, see page 179.

Work & School

What do you do?	**Vad sysslar du med?** vahd _sews_·lar deu meed
What are you studying?	**Vad läser du?** vahd _lai_·sehr deu
I'm studying...	**Jag läser...** yahg _lai_·sehr...
I work full time/ part time.	**Jag arbetar heltid/deltid.** yahg ahr·beh·tar hehl·teed/dehl·teed
I work at home.	**Jag arbetar hemifrån.** yahg ahr·beh·tar hehm·ih·froan
I'm unemployed	**Jag är arbetslös.** yahg air ar·behts·lus
Who do you work for?	**Vilken firma jobbar du på?** _vihl_·kehn _fihr_·ma _yohb_·ar deu p**oa**
I work for...	**Jag jobbar på...** yahg _yohb_·ar p**oa**...
Here's my business card.	**Här är mitt kort.** hair air miht koahrt

For Business Travel, see page 155.

Weather

What's the weather forecast for tomorrow?	**Vad är väderleksrapporten för imorgon?** *vahd air <u>vair</u>•dehr•<u>leeks</u>•ra•<u>pohr</u>•tehn furr ee•<u>mo</u>•ron*
What beautiful/ terrible weather!	**Vilket vackert/förskräckligt väder!** *<u>vihl</u>•keht <u>va</u>•kert/furr•<u>skrehk</u>•ligt <u>vair</u>•dehr*
It's...	**Det är...** *dee air...*
hot/cold	**varmt/kallt** *varmt/kahlt*
cool/warm	**svalt/varmt** *svahlt/varmt*
rainy/sunny	**regnigt/soligt** <u>rehng</u>•nihkt/<u>soal</u>•ikt
snowy/icy	**snöigt/halt** *snur•ikt/hahlt*
Do I need a jacket/ an umbrella?	**Behöver jag en jacka/ett paraply?** *beh•<u>hur</u>•ver yahg ehn <u>yah</u>•ka/eht pa•ra•<u>plew</u>*

For Temperature, see page 186.

ESSENTIAL

Would you like to go out for a drink/dinner?	**Har du lust att ta en drink/gå ut och äta?** *hahr deu luhst at tah ehn drihnk/goa eut ohk air•ta*
What are your plans for tonight/tomorrow?	**Vad har du för planer för ikväll/imorgon?** *vahd hahr deu furr plah•nehr furr ee•kvehl/ee•mo•ron*
Can I have your number?	**Kan jag få ditt telefonnummer?** *kan yahg foa diht teh•leh•foan•nuhm•ehr*
May I join you?	**Får jag göra dig sällskap?** *foar yahg yurra dihg sehl•skahp*
Can I buy you a drink?	**Får jag bjuda på en drink?** *foar yahg byeu•da poa ehn drihnk*
I like you.	**Jag gillar dig.** *yahg yihl•ar day*
I love you.	**Jag älskar dig.** *yahg ehl•skar day*

The Dating Game

Would you like to...?	**Har du lust att...?** *hahr deu luhst at...*
go out for coffee	**gå ut och ta en kopp kaffe** *goa eut ohk tah ehn kohp ka•fer*
go for a drink	**ta en drink** *tah ehn drihnk*
go out for a meal	**gå ut och äta** *goa eut ohk air•ta*
What are your plans for...?	**Vad har du för planer för...?** *vahd hahr deu furr plah•nehr furr...*
today	**idag** *ee•dahg*
tonight	**ikväll** *ee•kvehl*
tomorrow	**imorgon** *ee•mo•ron*
this weekend	**den här helgen** *dehn hair hehl•yehn*
Where would you like to go?	**Vart vill du gå?** *vart vihl deu goa*

I'd like to go to...	**Jag skulle vilja gå till.** *yahg <u>skuh</u>•ler <u>vihl</u>•ya*
	*g**oa** tihl…*
Do you like…?	**Tycker du om…?** *<u>tew</u>•kehr deu ohm…*
Can I have your number/e-mail?	**Kan jag få ditt nummer/din e-post?** *kan yahg f**oa** diht <u>nuhm</u>•ehr/dihn ee•<u>pohst</u>*
Are you on Facebook/Twitter?	**Finns du på Facebook/Twitter?** *fihns deu poa Facebook/Twitter*
Can I join you?	**Får jag följa med?** *f**oa**r yahg <u>furl</u>•ya meed*
You're very attractive.	**Du är väldigt snygg.** *deu air vehl•dihkt snewgg*
You look great!	**Vad du ser vacker ut!** *vahd deu seer <u>va</u>•kehr eut*
Shall we go somewhere quieter?	**Ska vi gå till ett lugnare ställe?** *skah vee g**oa** tihl eht <u>luhng</u>•na•rer <u>stehl</u>•ler*

For Communications, see page 49.

Accepting & Rejecting

Thank you. I'd love to.	**Tack, det vill jag gärna.** *tak dee vihl yahg <u>yair</u>•na*
Where should we meet?	**Var ska vi träffas?** *vahr skah vee <u>treh</u>•fas*
I'll meet you at the bar/your hotel.	**Vi träffas i baren/på ditt hotell.** *vee <u>treh</u>•fas ee <u>bahr</u>•en/p**oa** diht hoh•<u>tehl</u>*
I'll come by at…	**Jag kommer…** *yahg koh•mehr…*

What's your address?	**Vilken address har du?** *Vihl·kehn ahd·rehs hahr deu*
Thank you, but I'm busy.	**Tack, men jag är upptagen.** *tak men yahg air <u>uhp</u>·tah·gehn*
I'm not interested.	**Jag är inte intresserad.** *yahg air <u>in</u>·ter in·treh·<u>see</u>·rad*
Leave me alone, please!	**Kan du lämna mig ifred, tack!** *kan deu <u>lehm</u>·na may ee·<u>freed</u> tak*
Stop bothering me!	**Sluta störa mig!** *<u>sluh</u>·ta <u>stur</u>·ra may*

Getting Intimate

Can I hug/kiss you?	**Får jag krama/kysa dig?** *foar yahg <u>krah</u>·ma/<u>chews</u>·a day*
Yes.	**Ja.** *yah*
No.	**Nej.** *nay*
Stop!	**Stopp!** *stop*

Sexual Preferences

Are you gay?	**Är du gay?** *air deu gay*
I'm…	**Jag är…** *yahg air…*
heterosexual	**heterosexuell** <u>heh</u>·tehr·ro·sehk·shew·<u>ehl</u>
homosexual	**homosexuell** <u>hoh</u>·moa·sehk·shew·<u>ehl</u>
bisexual	**bisexuell** <u>bee</u>·sehk·shew·<u>ehl</u>
Do you like men/women?	**Gillar du män/kvinnor?** *yih·lahr deu mehn/kvih·nohr*

For Grammar, see page 175.

Leisure Time

ESSENTIAL

Where's the tourist information office?	**Var ligger turistinformationen?** *vahr lih•gehr teu•rihst•ihn•fohr•ma•shoan•ehn*
What are the main points of interest?	**Vad finns det för sevärdheter?** *vahd fihns dee furr see•vaird•hee•tehr*
Do you have tours in English?	**Finns det några turer på engelska?** *fihns dee noa•gra teu•rehr poa ehng•ehl•ska*
Can I have a map/ guide, please?	**Kan jag få en karta/guide, tack?** *kan yahg foa ehn kahr•ta/gujd tak*

Tourist Information

Do you have any information on…?	**Har ni information om…?** *hahr nee ihn•for•ma•shoan om…*
Can you recommend…?	**Kan ni rekommendera…?** *kan nee reh•koh•mehn dee•ra…*
a boat trip	**en båttur** *ehn boat•teur*
an excursion	**en rundtur** *ehn ruhnd•teur*
a sightseeing tour	**en sightseeingtur** *ehn sight•see•ihng•teur*

On Tour

I'd like to go on the tour to…	**Jag vill följa med på turen till…** *yahg vihl furl•ja meed poa teu•ren tihl…*
When's the next tour?	**När går nästa rundresa?** *nair goar nehsta ruhnd•rehsa*
Are there tours in English?	**Finns det någon tur på engelska?** *fihns dee noa•gohn teur poa ehng•ehl•ska*

There are tourist information offices in all large cities and towns. These are usually marked by a green sign with an **I**. For general information, Sweden's official tourism website is a good place to start. Here you can find information on accommodation, attractions and activities as well as cultural and historical information. Most cities have their own tourist boards and websites, where you can request brochures, maps and more prior to your arrival. Also look for **Stockholmskortet** (the Stockholm Card) if you will be spending several days in the city. For one fee, you have access to musems, events and transportation throughout the city. You can choose whether you want the card for 24, 48 or 72 hours. The equivalent in Göteborg is **Göteborgs Passet.**

Is there an English-speaking guide/audio guide?	**Finns det en engelsktalande guide/ljudguide?** _fihns deht ehn ehng·ehlsk·tah·lan·de gahyd/ aw·dee·oh gahyd_
What time do we leave/return?	**När åker vi/kommer vi tillbaka?** _nair <u>oak</u>·er vee/<u>koh</u>·mehr vee tihl·<u>bah</u>·ka_
We'd like to have a look at…	**Vi skulle vilja se…** _vee <u>skuh</u>·ler <u>vihl</u>·ya see…_
Can we stop here…?	**Kan vi stanna här…?** _kan vee <u>sta</u>·na hair…_
to take photographs	**för att ta foton** _furr at tah <u>foa</u>·tohn_
to buy souvenirs	**för att köpa souvenirer** _furr at <u>chur</u>·pa seu·veh·<u>nee</u>·rehr_
to use the toilets	**för att gå på toaletten** _furr at goa poa toa·ah·<u>leh</u>·tehn_
Is there access for the disabled?	**Finns det tillgång för rörelsehindrade?** _fihns d<u>ee</u> tihl·goang furr <u>rurr</u>·ehl·ser·<u>hihn</u>·dra·der_

For Tickets, see page 21.

Seeing the Sights

Where is...?	**Var ligger...?** *vahr lih·gehr...*
the battleground	**slagfältet** *slahg·fehl·teht*
the botanical garden	**botaniska trädgården** *boa·tan·ihs·ska traird·goar·dehn*
Where is...?	**Var ligger...?** *vahr lih·gehr...*
the castle	**slottet** *sloht·eht*
the downtown area	**centrum** *sehn·truhm*
the fountain	**fontänen** *fohn·tairn·ehn*
the library	**biblioteket** *bihb·lee·oa·teek·eht*
the market	**torget** *tohr·yeht*
the museum	**museet** *muh·see·eht*
the old town	**gamla stan** *gam·la stahn*
the opera house	**operan** *oap·eh·ran*
the palace	**slottet** *sloht·eht*
the park	**parken** *park·ehn*
the shopping area	**Et affärscentrumet** *eht a·ffairs·sehn·truhm·eht*
the town hall	**stadshuset** *stads·heus·eht*
Can you show me on the map?	**Kan du visa mig på kartan?** *kan deu vee·sa may poa kahr·tan*
It's...	**Det är...** *det air...*
amazing	**fantastiskt** *fan·ta·stihskt*
beautiful	**vackert** *va·kehrt*
boring	**trist** *trihst*
interesting	**intressant** *in·treh·sant*
magnificent	**storslaget** *stoar·slahg·eht*
romantic	**romantiskt** *roh·man·tihskt*
strange	**konstigt** *kohn·stihgt*
stunning	**förbluffande** *furr·bluh·fahnder*

terrible	**hemskt** *hehmskt*
ugly	**fult** *feult*
I (don't) like it.	**Jag tycker (inte) om den/det.** *yahg tew•kehr (in•ter) ohm dehn/dee*

For Asking Directions, see page 35.

For Grammar, see page 175.

Religious Sites

Where is...?	**Var är...?** *vahr air...*
the cathedral	**domkyrkan** *dohm•chewr•kahn*
the church	**kyrkan** *chewr•kan*
the mosque	**moskén** *mos•kehn*
the shrine	**altaret** *alt•a•reht*
the synagogue	**synagogan** *sihn•a•gohg•an*
the temple	**templet** *tehmp•leht*
What time is mass/ the service?	**Hur dags är mässan/gudstjänsten?** *heur daks air mehs•an/geuds•tjain•stehn*

ESSENTIAL

Where is the market/ mall [shopping centre]?	**Var ligger orget/affärscentrumet?** *vahr lih·gehr tohr·yeht/a·ffairs·sehn·truhm·eht*
I'm just looking.	**Jag tittar bara.** *yahg tih·tar bah·ra*
Can you help me?	**Kan du hjälpa mig?** *kan deu yehlp·a may*
I'm being helped.	**Jag får hjälp, tack.** *yahg foar yehlp tak*
How much does it cost?	**Hur mycket kostar det?** *heur mew·ker kos·tar det*
This/That one, thanks.	**Den här/där, tack.** *dehn hair/dair tak*
That's all, thanks.	**Det var allt, tack.** *dee vahr alt tak*
Where do I pay?	**Var kan jag betala?** *vahr kan yahg beh·tah·la*
I'll pay in cash/by credit card.	**Jag vill betala kontant/med kreditkort.** *yahg vihl beh·tah·la kohn·tant/meed kreh·deet·koart*
A receipt, please.	**Kvittot, tack.** *kvih·tot tak*

At the Shops

Where is…?	**Var finns…?** *vahr fihns…*
the antiques store	**antikaffären** *an·teek·a·ffair·ehn*
the bakery	**bageriet** *bahg·eh·ree·eht*
the bookstore	**bokhandeln** *book·han·dehln*
the clothing store	**klädaffären** *klaird·a·ffair·ehn*
the delicatessen	**delikatessaffären** *dehl·eh·ka·tehs·a·fair·ehn*
the department store	**varuhuset** *vahr·eu·heus·eht*
the health food store	**hälsokostaffären** *hehl·soa·kost·a·fair·ehn*

the jeweler	**juveleraren**	*yeu·veh·lee·rar·ehn*
the liquor store [off licence]	**systembolaget**	*sews·teem·boa·lahg·eht*
the market	**torget**	*tohr·yeht*
the pastry shop	**konditoriet**	*kohn·deh·toh·ree·eht*
the pharmacy [chemist]	**apoteket**	*a·poa·tee·keht*
the produce [grocery] store	**livsmedelsaffären**	*lihvs·mee·dehls·a·fair·ehn*
the shoe store	**skoaffären**	*skoa·a·fair·ehn*
the shopping mall [shopping centre]	**affärscentrumet**	*a·ffairs·sehn·truhm·eht*
the souvenir store	**souvenirbutiken**	*seu·veh·neer·buh·tee·kehn*
the supermarket	**snabbköpet**	*snab·chur·peht*

Although Sweden still has many small, specialty shops, **Köpcentrum** (malls) are becoming more and more common, especially in larger towns. Many chain and department stores, such as **Åhléns** and **Kappahl** and **Hennes & Mauritz**, have branches all over the country, all of which sell quality goods. In the well-established Stockholm department store **NK**, you can find almost anything, though it can be quite expensive. Designer goods can be found at **DesignTorget** in Stockholm. For traditional handicrafts look for signs with **hemslöjd** (handicraft); in Stockholm, these can be found at **Svensk Hemslöjd** and **Svenskt Hantverk** (traditional handicraft stores). Many towns have colorful markets, where you can buy anything from fresh fruit and vegetables to flowers and handicrafts. **Julmarknaden** (Christmas market) in Stockholm in the Old Town and **Skansen** (outdoor park and museum), are historic shopping areas.

Where is…?	**Var finns…?** *vahr fihns…*
the tobacconist	**tobaksaffären** <u>toa</u>·baks·a·<u>ffair</u>·ehn
the toy store	**leksaksaffären** <u>leek</u>·sahks·a·<u>fair</u>·ehn

Ask an Assistant

When do you open/ close?	**När öppnar/stänger ni?** *nair <u>uhp</u>·nar/ <u>stehng</u>·er nee*
Where is…?	**Var finns…?** *vahr fihns…*
the cashier [cash desk]	**kassan** <u>kah</u>·san
the escalator	**rulltrappan** <u>ruhl</u>·tra·pan
the elevator [lift]	**hissen** <u>his</u>·ehn
the fitting room	**provrummet** <u>proav</u>·ruhm·eht
the store directory [guide]	**informationen** in·for·ma·<u>shoa</u>·nehn
Can you help me?	**Kan du hjälpa mig?** *kan deu <u>yehl</u>·pa may*
I'm just looking.	**Jag tittar bara.** *yahg <u>tih</u>·tar <u>bah</u>·ra*
I'm being helped.	**Tack, jag får hjälp.** *tak yahg foar yehlp*
Do you have any…?	**Har ni några…?** *hahr nee <u>noa</u>·gra…*
Could you show me…?	**Kan du visa mig några…?** *kan deu <u>vee</u>·sa may <u>noa</u>·gra…*

YOU MAY HEAR...

Kan jag hjälpa er? *kan yahg yehl•pa her* — Can I help you?
Ett ögonblick, tack. *eht ur•gohn•blihk tak* — Just a moment, please.
Vad vill ni beställa? *vahd vihl nee beh•steh•la* — What would you like?
Något annat? *noa•goht an•nat* — Anything else?

Can you ship/wrap it?	**Kan du skicka/slå in det?** *kan deu shih•ka dee/sloa ihn dee*
How much does it cost?	**Hur mycket kostar det?** *heur mew•kerht kos•tar dee*
That's all, thanks.	**Det var allt, tack.** *dee vahr alt tak*

For Clothes & Accessories, see page 138.

For Meals & Cooking, see page 65.

Personal Preferences

I want something...	**Jag skulle vilja ha något...** *yahg skuh•ler vihl•ya hah noa•goht...*
cheap/expensive	**billigt/dyrt** *bihl•igt/dewyt*

YOU MAY SEE...

ÖPPET/STÄNGT	open/closed
STÄNGT FÖR LUNCH	closed for lunch
PROVRUM	fitting room
KASSÖR/KASSÖRSKA	cashier
ENDAST KONTANT	cash only
VI TAR KREDITKORT	credit cards accepted
AFFÄRSTID	business hours
UTGÅNG	exit

larger/smaller	**större/mindre** _sturr•er/mihn•drer_
from this region	**från denna region** _frohn deh•na regheoan_
Is it real?	**Är den äkta?** _air dehn aik•ta_
Could you show me this/that?	**Kan du visa mig den här/där?** _kan deu vee•sa may dehn hair/dair_
That's not quite what I want.	**Det är inte riktigt vad jag vill ha.** _dee air ihn•ter rihk•tikt vahd yahg vihl hah_
I don't like it.	**Jag tycker inte om det.** _yahg tew•kehr ihn•ter ohm dee_
That's too expensive.	**Det är för dyrt.** _dee air furr dewrt_
I'd like to think about it.	**Jag behöver tänka på det.** _Yahg beh•hur•vehr tehng•ka poa dee_
I'll take it.	**Jag tar den.** _yahg tahr dehn_

Paying & Bargaining

How much does it cost?	**Hur mycket kostar det?** _heur mew•ker kos•tar dee_
I'll pay...	**Jag betalar...** _yahg beh•tah•lar..._
in cash	**kontant** _kohn•tant_
by credit card	**med kreditkort** _meed kreh•deet•koart_
by traveler's check [cheque]	**med en resecheck** _meed ehn ree•seh•shehk_
The receipt, please.	**Kvittot, tack.** _kvih•toht tak_
That's too much.	**Det är för mycket.** _dee air furr mew•ker_
I'll give you...	**Jag kan ge er...** _yahg kan yee ehr..._
I only have...kronor.	**Jag har bara...kronor.** _yahg hahr bah•ra... kroa•nohr_
Is that your best price?	**Är det ditt bästa pris?** _air deht diht beh•sta prihs_
Can you give me a discount?	**Kan du ge mig rabatt?** _kan deu yee may ra•bat_

For Numbers, see page 179.

YOU MAY HEAR...

Hur vill ni betala? *heur vihl nee beh‧tah‧la*	How are you paying?
Ditt kreditkort har avvisats. *diht kreh‧dith‧koart hahr ahv‧veesahts*	Your credit card has been declined.
ID, tack. *ee‧deh, tak.*	ID, please.
Vi tar inte kreditkort. *Vee tahr ihnte kreh‧diht‧koart*	We don't accept credit cards.
Bara kontanter, tack. *bah‧ra kohn‧tan‧tehr tak*	Cash only, please.
Har du mindre växel? *hahr deu mihn‧drer vehx‧ehl*	Do you have any smaller change?

Making a Complaint

I'd like...	**Jag skulle vilja...** *yahg skuh‧ler vihl‧ya...*
to exchange this	**byta den här** *bew‧ta dehn hair*
to return this	**återlämna den här** *oa‧tehr‧lehm‧na dehn hair*
a refund	**ha pengarna tillbaka** *hah pehng‧ar‧na tihl‧bah‧ka*
to see the manager	**få träffa butikschefen** *foa treh‧fa beu‧teeks‧sheef‧ehn*

Services

Can you recommend...?	**Kan du rekommendera...?** *kan deu reh‧koh‧mehn‧dee‧ra...*
a barber	**en herrfrisör** *ehn hair‧fri‧surr*
a dry cleaner	**en kemtvätt** *ehn shehm‧tveht*
a hairdresser	**en damfrisör** *ehn dahm‧free‧surr*
a laundromat [launderette]	**en snabbtvätt** *ehn snab‧tveht*
a nail salon	**en nagelvårdssalong** *ehn nah‧gehl‧voards‧sa‧loang*

a spa	**ett spa** *eht spah*
a travel agency	**en resebyrå** *ehn <u>ree</u>·seh·<u>bew</u>·roa*
Can you…this?	**Kan ni…den här?** *kan nee…dehn hair*
alter	**ändra på** *<u>ehn</u>·dra poa*
clean	**göra ren** *yur·ra reen*
mend	**laga** *<u>lah</u>·ga*
press	**stryka** *<u>strew</u>·ka*
When will it be ready?	**När blir det klart?** *nair bleer dee klahrt*

Hair & Beauty

I'd like…	**Jag vill…** *yahg vihl…*
an appointment for today/ tomorrow	**boka en tid till idag/imorgon** *<u>boa</u>·ka ehn teed tihl ee·dahg/ee·<u>mo</u>·ron*
some colour/ highlights	**färg/slingor** *fehry/slihng·ohr*
my hair styled/ blow-dried	**få en ny frisyr/föning** *foa ehn new free·<u>sewr</u>/ funeeng*
a hair cut	**få en klippning** *foa ehn <u>klihp</u>·nihng*
an eyebrow/ a bikini wax	**en vaxning av ögonbrynen/bikinilinjen** *ehn <u>vaks</u>·nihng afv <u>ur</u>·gonn·brew·nehn/ beh·<u>kee</u>·nee·<u>leen</u>·yehn*
a facial	**en ansiktsbehandling** *ehn <u>an</u>·sihkts·beh·<u>hand</u>·lihng*

Spas and wellness centers are becoming increasingly popular.
There are many to choose from, both in urban and rural areas.
It is possible to find spas that offer everything from traditional
massage, such as the Swedish massage, which focuses on circulation
and relaxation, to yoga, exercise and more. Some are even eco-friendly.
Many spas and health centers also have gyms, pools and saunas.

a manicure/ pedicure	**en manikyr/pedikyr**	*ehn ma•nee•kewr/ pehd•ee•kewr*
a (sports) massage	**(tränings) massage**	*(trair•nihngs•) ma•sahsh*
a trim, please...	**en klippning, tack...**	*ehn klihp•nihng, tak*
Don't cut it too short.	**Klipp det inte för kort.**	*klihp dee ihn•ter furr koart*
Shorter here.	**Kortare här.**	*koar•ta•rer hair*
Do you do...?	**Ger ni...?**	*yehr nee...*
acupuncture	**akupunktur**	*a•keu•puhnk•teur*
aromatherapy	**aroma-terapi**	*a•roa•ma•teh•ra•pee*
oxygen treatment	**syrebehandling**	*sew•reh•beh•hand•lihng*
Is there a sauna?	**Finns det bastu?**	*fihns dee bas•teu*

Antiques

How old is this?	**Hur gammalt är det här?**	*heur gam•alt air dee hair*
Do you have anything from the ... era?	**Har ni något från ... perioden?** *hahr nee noh•goht frohn ... per•eeoh•dehn*	
Will I have problems with customs?	**Får jag problem i tullen?** *foar yahg proa•bleem ee tuh•lehn*	
Is there a certificate of authenticity?	**Finns det ett äkthetsbevis?** *fihns dee eht ehkt•heets•beh•vees*	
Can you ship/wrap it?	**Kan ni skicka/packa in det?** *kahn nee shih•ka/ paka ihn deht*	

Clothing

I'd like...	**Jag skulle vilja ha...**	*yahg skuh•ler vihl•ya hah...*
Can I try this on?	**Kan jag prova den här?**	*kan yahg proa•va dehn hair*

YOU MAY SEE...

HERRKLÄDER	men's clothing
DAMKLÄDER	women's clothing
BARNKLÄDER	children's clothing

YOU MAY HEAR...

Du klär jättebra i den. *Deu klair jai·teh·brah i dehn*

That looks great on you.

Hur sitter den? *huhr sih·tehr dehn*

How does it fit?

Vi har inte din storlek. *Vee hahr ihnte deen stohr·lehk*

We don't have your size.

It doesn't fit.	**Den passar inte.** *dehn pas·ar ihn·ter*	
It's too...	**Den är för...** *dehn air furr...*	
big	**stor** *stoar*	
small	**liten** *lee·tehn*	
short	**kort** *kort*	
long	**lång** *loang*	
tight	**liten** *leetehn*	
loose	**stor** *stohr*	
Do you have this in size...?	**Har ni den här i storlek...?** *hahr nee dehn hair ee stoar·leek...*	
Do you have this in a bigger/smaller size?	**Har ni den här i en större/en mindre storlek?** *hahr nee dehn hair ee ehn stur·re/ ehn mihn·drer stoar·leek*	

For Numbers, see page 179.

Colors

I'm looking for something in...	**Jag söker något i...** *yahg sur·ker noa·goht ee...*
beige	**beige** *beesh*
black	**svart** *svart*
blue	**blått** *bloat*

brown	**brunt** *breunt*	
gray	**grått** *groat*	
green	**grönt** *grurnt*	
orange	**orange** *oa·ransh*	
pink	**rosa** <u>roa</u>·sa	
purple	**lila** <u>lee</u>·la	
red	**rött** *ruhrt*	
white	**vitt** *vit*	
yellow	**gult** *geult*	
I'm looking for something in…	**Jag söker något i…** *yahg <u>sur</u>·ker <u>noa</u>·goht ee…*	

Clothes & Accessories

a backpack	**ryggsäck** <u>rewg</u>·sehk
a belt	**skärp** *shairp*
a bikini	**bikini** *bih·<u>kee</u>·nee*
a blouse	**blus** *bleus*
a bra	**behå** <u>beh</u>·hoa
briefs [underpants]	**kalsonger [underbyxor]** *khal·sohn·gehr [uhn·dehr·bew·xohr]*
panties	**trosor** *troh·sohr*
a coat	**rock** *rohk*
a dress	**klänning** <u>klehn</u>·ihng
a hat	**hatt** *hat*
a jacket	**jacka** <u>ya</u>·ka
jeans	**jeans** *jeens*
pajamas	**pyjamas** *pew·<u>ya</u>·mas*
pants [trousers]	**byxor** <u>bewx</u>·ohr
panty hose [tights]	**strumpbyxor** <u>struhmp</u>·bewx·ohr
a purse [handbag]	**handväska** <u>hand</u>·vehs·ka
a raincoat	**regnkappa** <u>rehngn</u>·kap·a

a scarf	**halsduk** _hals_•d**eu**k
a shirt	**skjorta** _shoar_•ta
shorts	**shorts** shohrts
a skirt	**kjol** choal
socks	**sockar** _soh_•kar
stockings	**strumpor** stuhm•pohr
a suit (jacket and pants)	**kostym** kos•_tewm_
a suit (jacket and skirt)	**dräkt** drehkt
sunglasses	**solglasögon** _soal_•glahs•**ur**•gohn
a sweater	**tröja** _trur_•ya
a sweatshirt	**sweatshirt** _sweat_•shirt swimming
swimming trunks	**badbyxor** _bahd_•bewx•ohr
a swimsuit	**baddräkt** _bahd_•drehkt
a T-shirt	**T-skjorta** _tee_•shoarta
a tie	**slips** slihps
underpants (men's/women's)	**kalsonger/trosor** kal•_soang_•ehr/_troa_•sohr
underwear	**underkläder** uhn•dehr•klai•dehr

Fabric

I'd like...	**Jag skulle vilja ha...** yahg _skuh_•ler _vihl_•ya hah...
cotton	**bomull** _boam_•uhl
denim	**denim** _dehn_•ihm
lace	**spets** spehts
leather	**läder** _lair_•der
linen	**linne** _lih_•ner
silk	**siden** _see_•dehn
wool	**ull** uhl
Is it machine washable?	**Kan det tvättas i maskin?** kan dee _tveht_•as ee ma•_sheen_

Shoes

I'd like…	**Jag skulle vilja ha…** *yahg <u>skuh</u>•ler <u>vihl</u>•ya hah…*
high-heeled/	**högklackade/lågklackade skor**
flat shoes	*<u>hurg</u>•klak•a•der/<u>loag</u>•klak•a•der sk<u>oa</u>r*
boots	**stövlar** *<u>stuhv</u>•lar*
I'd like…	**Jag skulle vilja ha…** *yahg <u>skuh</u>•ler <u>vihl</u>•ya hah…*
loafers	**loafers** *<u>loa</u>•fers*
sandals	**sandaler** *san•<u>dahl</u>•ehr*
shoes	**skor** *sk<u>oa</u>r*
slippers	**tofflor** *<u>toff</u>•lohr*
sneakers	**träningsskor** *<u>trair</u>•nihngs•sk<u>oa</u>r*
In size…	**I storlek…** *ee <u>stoar</u>•leek…*

For Numbers, see page 179.

Sizes

Small (S)	**liten** *<u>leet</u>•ehn*
Medium (M)	**medium** *<u>mee</u>•dee•uhm*
large (L)	**stor** *st<u>oa</u>r*
extra large (XL)	**extra stor** *<u>ehx</u>•tra st<u>oa</u>r*
petite	**petite** *peh•<u>teet</u>*
plus size	**plus-storlek** *<u>pleus</u>•st<u>oa</u>r•leek*

Newsagent & Tobacconist

Do you sell English language books/ newspapers?	**Säljer ni böcker/tidningar på engelska?** <u>sehl</u>·yehr nee <u>bur</u>·kehr/<u>teed</u>·nihng·ar **po**a ehng·ehl·ska
I'd like...	**Jag skulle vilja ha...** yahg <u>skuh</u>·ler <u>vihl</u>·ya hah...
candy [sweets]	**godis [sötsaker]** goa·dihs [sut·sahk·ehr]
some chewing gum	**tuggummi** <u>tuhg</u>·guh·mee
a chocolate bar	**en chokladkaka** ehn shohk·lahd·kahka
some cigars	**några cigarrer** noa·gra see·<u>gahr</u>·er
a pack/carton of cigarettes	**ett paket/en limpa cigaretter** eht pak·<u>eht</u>/ ehn <u>lihm</u>·pa sih·ga·<u>reht</u>·her
a lighter	**en tändare** ehn <u>tehn</u>·da·rehr
a magazine	**en veckotidning** ehn veh·koa·<u>teed</u>·nihng
matches	**tändstickor** <u>tehnd</u>·stik·ohr
a newspaper	**en tidning** ehn <u>teed</u>·nihng
a pen	**en penna** ehn peh·na
a postcard	**ett vykort** eht <u>vew</u>·koart
a road/town map of...	**en vägkarta/stadskarta över...** ehn <u>vairg</u>·kahr·ta/<u>stats</u>·kahr·ta <u>ur</u>·vehr...
some stamps	**några frimärken** noa·gra <u>free</u>·mair·kehn

Photography

I'm looking for... camera.	**Jag skulle vilja köpa...kamera.** yahg <u>skuh</u>·ler <u>vihl</u>·ya <u>chur</u>·pa... <u>kah</u>·meh·ra
an automatic	**en automatisk** ehn ah·toa·<u>mah</u>·tihsk
a digital	**en digital** ehn dih·gih·<u>tahl</u>
a disposable	**en engångs** ehn <u>een</u>·goangs
I'd like...	**Jag skulle vilja ha...** yahg <u>skuh</u>·ler <u>vihl</u>·ya hah...
a battery	**ett batteri** eht ba·teh·<u>ree</u>
a digital print	**ett digitalt kort** eht dih·gih·<u>tahlt</u> koart
a memory card	**ett minneskort** eht <u>mihn</u>·ehs·koart

Can I print digital photos here?	**Kan jag skriva ut digitala foton här?**
	kan yahg skree•va eut dih•gih•tah•la foh•toan hair

Souvenirs

candlesticks	**ljusstakar** *yeus•stah•kar*
Christmas decorations	**juldekorationer** *yeul•dehk•oh•ra•shoan•ehr*
clogs	**träskor** *trair•skoar*
crystal (glass)	**kristallglas** *kree•stal•glahs*
a Dala horse (red wooden horse)	**en dalahäst** *ehn dah•la•hehst*
dolls	**dockor** *dok•oar*
glassware	**glasföremål** *glahs•furr•reh•moal*
handicrafts	**hemslöjd** *hehm•sluhyd*
horn work	**något i horn** *noa•goht ee hoarn*
jewelry	**smycken** *smew•kehn*
porcelain	**porslin** *pohrsh•leen*
pottery	**keramik** *cheh•ra•meek*
reindeer antlers	**renhorn** *reen•hoarn*
Sami handicrafts	**sameslöjd** *sah•meh•sluhyd*
smoked salmon	**rökt lax** *rurkt lax*
a tablecloth	**en duk** *ehn deuk*
textiles	**textil** *tehx•teel*
wood carvings	**träfigurer** *trair•fih•geu•rehr*
a wooden knife	**en träkniv** *ehn trair•kneev*
a wooden spoon	**en träsked** *ehn trair•sheed*
Can I see this/that?	**Får jag se på den här/där?** *foar yahg she poa dehn hair/dair*
The one in the window/display case.	**Den i fönstret/vitrinet.** *dehn ee furn•streht/vi•treen•eht*
I'd like…	**Jag skulle vilja ha…** *yahg skuh•ler vihl•ya hah…*
a battery	**ett batteri** *eht ba•teh•ree*

a bracelet	**ett armband** *eht arm•band*
a brooch	**en brosch** *ehn broash*
earrings	**örhängen** *ur•hehng•ehn*
a necklace	**ett halsband** *eht hals•band*
a ring	**en ring** *ehn rihng*
a watch	**en armbandsklocka** *ehn arm•bands•kloh•ka*
copper	**koppar** *kohpp•ar*

When it comes to souvenirs, whether you are looking for something traditional or modern, you are sure to find just the thing in Sweden. **Träslöjd** (woodwork), **hemslöjd** (handicrafts), **keramik** (ceramics) and Swedish crystal are popular, traditional souvenirs. The **dalahäst** (Dala horse) is perhaps one of the most famous and ubiquitous souvenirs; traditionally, its color is a reddish-orange, but the horses can now be found in a wide range of colors and sizes. Sweden is known for its design, which is evident in its selection of **porslin** (fine china) and ceramics. Some well-known manufacturers include **Höganäs Keramik** and **Rörstrand**, the latter being the second oldest porcelain manufacturer in Europe, founded in 1746. Sweden is also famous for its glass and crystal, both with respect to design and to quality. **Glasriket** (the kingdom of glass) located in Småland, in southeastern Sweden, has around 15 glass factories, including some of the most famous glassworks in Sweden, such as **Kosta Boda**, **Orrefors** and **Nybro**. Factory tours are often available. In addition to the traditional Swedish handicrafts mentioned above, **sameslöjd** (**Sámi** handicraft) is something that should not be overlooked. The **Sámi** are known for their beautiful crafts, which include jewelry and knives carved from reindeer antlers, jewelry made from beaded pewter and reindeer leather as well as a wide range of clothing in reindeer leather and different types of fur.

crystal (quartz)	**kristall** *krihs·tall*
diamond	**diamant** *dee·a·mant*
white/yellow gold	**vitt/rött guld** *viht/rurtt geuld*
pearl	**pärla** *pair·la*
I'd like...	**Jag skulle vilja ha...** *yahg skuh·ler vihl·ya hah...*
pewter	**tenn** *teen*
platinum	**platina** *plah·tee·na*
sterling silver	**äkta silver** *ehk·ta sihl·vehr*
Is this real?	**Är den här äkta?** *air dehn hair ehk·ta*
Can you engrave it?	**Kan ni gravera den?** *kan nee gra·vee·ra dehn*

Sport & Leisure

ESSENTIAL

When's the game?	**När börjar matchen?** *nair bur·yar ma·shchehn*
Where's...?	**Var ligger...?** *vahr lih·gehr...*
the beach	**stranden** *stran·dehn*
Where's...?	**Var ligger...?** *vahr lih·gehr...*
the park	**parken** *park·ehn*
the pool	**simbassängen** *sihm·ba·sehng·ehn*
Is it safe to swim/ dive here?	**Kan man simma/dyka här utan risk?** *kan man sihmm·a/dew·ka hair eu·tan rihsk*
Can I rent [hire] golf clubs?	**Kan man hyra golfklubbor?** *kan man hew·ra gohlf·kluh·bohr*
How much per hour?	**Vad kostar det per timme?** *vahd kos·tar dee pair tihm·er*
How far is it to...?	**Hur långt är det till...?** *heur loangt air dee tihl...*
Can you show me on the map?	**Kan du visa mig på kartan?** *kan deu vee sa may poa kahr·tan*

Sports and recreation are popular, and there are excellent sports facilities everywhere, ranging from **golf** (golf), **fiske** (fishing), **tennis** (tennis) and **fotboll** (soccer) to **skidåkning** (skiing) and **ishockey** (ice hockey). Tourist offices should have contact information for the various sports facilities in your area. Swedes also love the great outdoors, and the country has much to offer when it comes to **bergklättring** (mountain climbing), **vandring** (hiking), **ridsport** (horsebackriding), **cykelåkning** (cycling), **paddla kanot** (canoeing) and **segling** (boating). Whether you are looking for a day hike or planning a longer trip, some great choices include **Kebnekaise**, which is Sweden's highest mountain, **Kungsleden**, **Bohusleden** or **Padjelantleden**. There are a lot of options for cyclists, both amateurs and professionals, and popular cycle routes include **Kustlinjen** and **Sverigeleden**.

Watching Sport

When's…?	**När börjar…?** *nair bur·yar…*
the baseball game	**basebollmatchen** *base·bohl·mat·shehn*
the basketball game	**basketbollmatchen** *bahs·keht·bohl·ma·shchehn*
the boxing match	**boxningsmatchen** *boax·nihngs·matsh·ehn*
the cricket game	**cricketspelet** *cricket·matsh·ehn*
the cycling race	**cykeltävlingen** *sew·kehl·taiv·lihng·ehn*
the golf tournament	**golfspelet** *golf·spee·leht*
the soccer [football] game	**fotbollsmatchen** *foat·bohls·ma·shchehn*
the tennis match	**tennismatchen** *tehn·ihs·ma·shchehn*
the volleyball game	**volleybollspelet** *voh·lee·bohl·spee·leht*

Which teams are playing?	**Vilka lag spelar?** _vihl•ka lahg _spee•_lar
Where's the stadium?	**Var ligger idrottsarenan?** _vahr lih•gehr ee•drohts•a•ree•nan_
Where's the horsetrack/racetrack?	**Var finns hästkapplöpnings/kapplöpningsbanan?** _Vahr fihns hehst•kap•luhp•nihngs/kahp•luhp•nihgs•bahn•an_
Where can I place a bet?	**Var kan jag spela lotto?** _vahr kan yahg _spee•_la _loh•_toa_

Playing Sport

Is there…nearby?	**Finns det…i närheten?** _fihns dee… ee _nair•_hee•_ten_
a golf course	**en golfbana** _ehn _gohlf•_bah•na_
a gym	**ett gym** _eht yim_
a park	**en park** _ehn park_
a tennis court	**en tennisbana** _ehn _tehn•ihs•bah•nohr_
How much per…?	**Hur mycket kostar det per…?** _heur _mew•_ker _kos•_tar d_ee_ pair…_
day	**dag** _dahg_
hour	**timme** _tihm•er_
game	**spel** _speel_
round	**runda** _ruhn•da_

Can I rent [hire]…?	**Kan man hyra…?** *kan man <u>hew</u>·ra…*
golf clubs	**klubbor** *<u>kluhb</u>·ohr*
equipment	**utrustning** *<u>eut</u>·ruhst·nihng*
a racket	**en racket** *ehn <u>ra</u>·keht*

At the Beach/Pool

Where's the beach/pool?	**Var är stranden/simbassängen?** *vahr air <u>stran</u>·dehn/<u>sihm</u>·ba·<u>sehng</u>·ehn*
Is there a…here?	**Finns det…här?** *fihns dee…hair*
a kiddie [paddling] pool	**en barnbassäng** *ehn <u>bahrn</u>·bah·<u>sehng</u>*
an indoor/outdoor pool	**en inomhuspool/utomhuspool** *ehn <u>in</u>·ohm·heus·poal/<u>eut</u>·ohm·heus·poal*
a lifeguard	**en livräddare** *<u>leev</u>·rehd·a·rer*
Is it safe to swim/dive?	**Kan man simma/dyka här utan risk?** *Kan man <u>sihm</u>·a/<u>dew</u>·ka hair <u>eu</u>·tan rihsk*
Is it safe for children?	**Är det barnsäkert?** *air dee <u>bahrn</u>·sair·kert*
I want to hire…	**Jag skulle vilja hyra…** *yahg <u>skuh</u>·ker <u>vihl</u>·ya <u>hew</u>·ra…*
a deck chair	**en solstol** *ehn <u>soal</u>·stoal*
diving equipment	**dykutrustning** *dewk·uht·ruhst·nihng*

A significant portion of the Swedish coastline is rough, covered with granite rocks and cliffs and dotted with beaches. Most of the sandy beaches are found in the south and on the southwest coasts. Around Stockholm you can swim and dive from the small islands in the archipelago — and you can even swim in the water around Stockholm itself. Inland lakes, coastal areas and the popular archipelagos of Stockholm and the West Coast are perfect for boaters, and canoeists and kayakers alike.

a jet ski	**en jetski** *ehn jeht•skee*
a motorboat	**en motorbåt** *ehn moa•tor•boat*
a rowboat	**en roddbåt** *ehn rohd•boat*
snorkeling equipment	**snorklingsutrustning** *snoh•rklihngs•uht•ruhst•nihng*
a surfboard	**en surfbräda** *ehn suhrf•brair•da*
a towel	**en handduk** *ehn hand•deuk*
an umbrella	**en solparasol** *ehn soal•pa•ra•sohl*
water skis	**vattenskidor** *va•tehrn•shee•dohr*
a windsurfer	**en vindsurfare** *ehn vihnd•suhr•fa•reh*

For Traveling with Children, see page 157.

Winter Sports

A lift pass for a day/ five days, please.	**Ett liftpass för en dag/för fem dagar, tack.** *eht lihft•pas furr ehn dahg/furr fehm dahg•ar tak*
Where's the ice rink?	**Var ligger isbanan?** *vahr lee•gehr ihs•bahn•an*
Are there lessons?	**Kan man få lektioner?** *kan man foa lehk•shoa•nehr*

Swedes grow up with skiing: cross-country in the south and downhill in the north. There are many excellent ski resorts in the north, offering superb skiing and first-class facilities. Many hotels offer three- to seven-day package deals, including transportation and accommodation. In June, try **Riksgränsen** for a taste of skiing in the midnight sun.

Långfärdsbussar (long-distance buses) are efficient, relatively cheap and run daily to all major towns and resorts. Most of the major ski resorts also offer other winter sport activities like snowmobile safaris, snowshoeing and dog sledding tours. **Ishotellet** (Ice Hotel), though not a ski resort specifically, does offer several of these activities.

YOU MAY SEE...

DRAGLIFT	drag lift
ÄGGLIFT	cable car
STOLLIFT	chair lift
NYBÖRJARE	novice
MELLANNIVÅ	intermediate
AVANCERAD	expert
SPÅRET STÄNGD	trail [piste] closed

How much?	**Hur mycket?** *huhr mew•keh*
I'm a beginner.	**Jag är nybörjare.** *yahg air new•bur•yah•reh*
I'm experienced.	**Jag har erfarenhet.** *yahg hahr air•fah•rehn•heet*
I'd like to hire...	**Jag skulle vilja hyra...** *yahg skuh•ler vihl•ya hew•ra...*
boots	**skidpjäxor** *sheed•pyeaix•ohr*
a helmet	**en hjälm** *ehn yehlm*
ice skates	**skridskor** *skrih•skohr*
poles	**stavar** *stah•var*
skis	**skidor** *shee•dohr*
a snowboard	**en snowboard** *ehn snow•board*
snowshoes	**pjäxor** *pyaix•ohr*
These are too big/small.	**De här är för stora/små.** *dehm hair air furr stoa•ra/smoa*
A trail [piste] map, please.	**En karta över spåren, tack.** *ehn kahr•ta ur•vehr spoa•rehn tak*

Out in the Country

I'd like a map of...	**Jag skulle vilja ha en karta över...** *yahg skuh•ler vihl•ya hah ehn kahr•ta ur•vehr...*
this region	**denna region** *dehn•a reh•gioan*

walking routes	**vandringsleder**	_van·drihngs·lee·dehr_
cycle routes	**cykeleder**	_sew·kehl·lee·dehr_
the trails	**spåren**	_spoa·rehn_
Is it easy/difficult?	**Är det lätt/svårt?**	_air dee leht/svoart_
Is it far/steep?	**Är det långt/brant?**	_air dee loangt/brant_
How far is it to…?	**Hur långt är det till…?**	_heur loangt air dee tihl…_
Can you show me on the map?	**Kan du visa mig på kartan?**	_kan deu vee·sa may poa kahr·tan_
I'm lost.	**Jag har kommit vilse.**	_yahg hahr koh·miht vihl·ser_
Where's…?	**Var ligger…?**	_vahr lih·gehr…_
the bridge	**bron**	_broan_
the cave	**grottan**	_groht·an_
the cliff	**klippa**	_klihp·an_
the farm	**bondgården**	_boand·goard·ehn_
the field	**åkern**	_oak·ern_
the footpath	**fotvandringsleden**	_foat·vand·rihngs·lee·dehn_
the forest	**skogen**	_skoag·ehn_
the hill	**berget**	_behr·yeht_
the lake	**sjön**	_shurn_
the mountain	**berget**	_behr·yeht_
the mountain pass	**bergspasset**	_berys·pas·eht_
the mountain range	**bergskedjan**	_berys·chee·dyan_
the nature reserve	**naturreservatet**	_na·teur·res·her·vah·teht_
the panorama	**panoraman**	_pan·o·rah·man_
the park	**parken**	_park·ehn_
the path	**stigen**	_stee·gehn_
Where's…?	**Var ligger…?**	_vahr lih·gehr…_
the peak	**toppen**	_tohp·ehn_
the picnic area/ rest area	**picknickområdet/rastplatsen**	_pihk·nihk·ohm·roa·det/rast·plats·ehn_

the pond	**dammen** *dah·mehn*
the river	**floden** *<u>float</u>·ehn*
the sea	**havet** *<u>hafv</u>·eht*
the hot spring	**den varma källan** *dehn var·ma cheh·lan*
the valley	**dalen** *<u>dahl</u>·ehn*
the viewpoint	**utsiktspunkten** *<u>eut</u>·sihkts·peunk·tehn*
the village	**byn** *bewn*
the vineyard	**vinodlingen** *vihn·ohd·lihng·ehn*
the waterfall	**vattenfallet** *<u>va</u>·tehrn·fal*

Going Out

ESSENTIAL

Do you have a program of events?	**Har ni ett evenemangsprogram?** *hahr nee eht eh·vehn·eh·<u>mangs</u>·proa·gram*
What's playing at the movies [cinema] tonight?	**Vad visas på bio ikväll?** *vahd <u>vee</u>·sas poa <u>bee</u>·oa ee·<u>kvehl</u>*
Where's…?	**Var ligger…?** *vahr <u>lih</u>·gehr…*
the downtown area	**centrum** *<u>sehn</u>·truhm*
the bar	**baren** *<u>bah</u>·rehn*
the dance club	**diskoteket** *dis·koh·<u>tee</u>·keht*

Entertainment

Can you recommend…?	**Kan du rekommendera…?** *kan deu reh·koh·mehn·<u>dee</u>·ra…*
a concert	**en konsert** *ehn kohn·<u>sair</u>*
a movie	**en film** *ehn film*

an opera	**en opera** *ehn <u>oa</u>·peh·ra*
a play	**en teaterpjäs** *ehn tee·<u>ah</u>·tehr·pjais*
When does it start/ end?	**När börjar/slutar den?** *nair <u>bur</u>·yar/<u>sleu</u>·tar dehn*
What's the dress code?	**Vilken klädsel gäller?** *<u>vihl</u>·kehn klaid·sehl <u>gehl</u>·lehr*
I like…	**Jag tycker om…** *yahg <u>tew</u>·kehr ohm…*
classical music	**klassisk musik** *<u>klas</u>·isk meu·<u>seek</u>*
folk music	**folkmusik** *<u>folk</u>·meu·<u>seek</u>*
jazz	**jazz** *yas*
pop music	**popmusik** *<u>pop</u>·meu·<u>seek</u>*
rap	**rap** *rap*

For Tickets, see page 21.

YOU MAY HEAR…

Stäng av mobiltelefonen, tack. *stehng afv mo·<u>beel</u>·teh·leh·<u>foa</u>·nen tak*

Turn off your cell [mobile] phones, please.

Nightlife

What's there to do at night?	**Vad kan man göra på kvällarna?** *vahd kan man <u>yur</u>·ra poa <u>kvehl</u>·ar·na*
Can you recommend…?	**Kan du rekommendera…?** *kan deu reh·koh·mehn·<u>dee</u>·ra…*
a bar	**en bar** *ehn bahr*
a casino	**ett kasino** *eht ka·<u>see</u>·noh*
a dance club	**ett diskotek** *eht dis·koh·<u>tehk</u>*
a gay club	**en gayklubb** *ehn <u>gay</u>·kluhb*
a jazz club	**en jazzklubb** *ehn <u>yas</u>·kluhb*

a club with local music	**en klubb med lokal musik** *ehn kluhb meed lo-kahl meu-seek*
a nightclub	**en nattklubb** *ehn nat-kluhb*
Is there live music?	**Spelar man livemusik där?** *spee-lar man live-meu-seek dair*
How do I get there?	**Hur kan jag komma dit?** *heur kan yahg koh-ma deet*
Is there a cover charge?	**Är det kuvertavgift?** *air de keu-vair-afv-yihft*
Let's go dancing.	**Vi går ut och dansar.** *vee goar eut ohk dan-sar*
Is this area safe at night?	**Är detta område säkert på natten?** *ehr deh-ta ohm-roh-deh seh-kehrt poh na-tehn*

Sweden has produced several world famous pop and rock bands, and music is an important part of contemporary culture and entertainment. The government generously supports independent musicians, as well as smaller music groups, orchestras and symphonies. In larger cities and towns you'll easily find concerts and performances to attend, and information should be listed at the tourist office or its webpage regarding upcoming concerts and events. If you are traveling in Sweden during the summer, attending a music festival is an unforgettable experience. **The Peace & Love Festival** in Borlänge, just two hours from Stockholm, is popular among the younger crowd. Stockholm is home to **Ung08**, which is Europe's largest youth festival, geared toward 13-19 year olds. **The Hultsfred Festival**, in southern Sweden, is the oldest and largest festival. There are also a host of other music festivals covering everything from folk music, to pop and jazz.

Special
Requirements

Business Travel

ESSENTIAL

I'm here on business.	**Jag är här på affärsresa.** *yahg air hair poa a·fairs·ree·sa*
Here's my business card.	**Här är mitt kort.** *hair air miht koart*
Can I have your card?	**Kan jag få ditt kort?** *kan yahg foa diht koart*
I have a meeting with...	**Jag har ett möte med...** *yahg hahr eht mur·ter meed...*
Where's...?	**Var ligger...?** *vahr lih·gehr...*
the business center	**businesscentret** *bihs·nihs·sehn·treht*
the convention hall	**kongresshallen** *kohn·grehs·ha·lehn*
the meeting room	**konferensrummet** *kohn·feh·rans·ruhm·eht*

On Business

I'm here to attend...	**Jag är här för att delta i...** *yahg air hair furr at deel·tah ee...*
a seminar	**ett seminarium** *eht sehm·i·nah·ree·uhm*
a conference	**en konferens** *ehn kohn·fehr·ans*
a meeting	**ett sammanträde** *eht sam·an·trai·der*
My name is...	**Jag heter...** *yahg hee·ter...*
May I introduce my colleague...	**Får jag presentera min kollega...** *foar yahg prehs·ehn·tee·ra mihn koh·lee·ga...*
Nice to meet you.	**Trevligt att träffas.** *treev·ligt at trehf·as*
I have a meeting/an appointment with...	**Jag har ett möte/en träff med...** *yahg hahr eht mut·eh/ehn trehf·mehd*
I'm sorry I'm late.	**Ursäkta för att jag är sen.** *eur·shehk·ta furr at yahg air sehn*

I'd like an interpreter.	**Jag behöver en tolk.** *yahg beh·hur·ver ehn tohlk*
You can reach me at the…Hotel.	**Du kan nå mig på hotell…** *deu kan noa may poa ho·tehl…*
I'm here until…	**Jag stannar till…** *yahg stan·ar tihl…*
I need to…	**Jag behöver…** *yahg beh·hur·ver…*
make a call	**ringa ett samtal** *rihng·a eht sam·tahl*
make a photocopy	**göra en kopia** *gur·ra ehn koh·pee·ya*

YOU MAY HEAR…

Har ni bokat tid? *hahr nee boa·kat teed*	Do you have an appointment?
Med vem? *meed vehm*	With whom?
Han/Hon sitter i möte. *han/hoan sih·ter ee mur·ter*	He/She is in a meeting.
Ett ögonblick, tack. *eht ur·gohn·blik tak*	One moment, please.
Varsågod och sitt. *Vahr·soa·gohd ohk siht*	Have a seat.
Vill du ha något att dricka? *Vihl deu hah nohgoht at drih·ka*	Would you like something to drink?
Tack för att ni kom. *tak furr at nee kom*	Thank you for coming.

send an e-mail	**skicka e-post** _shihk·a ee·pohst_
send a fax	**skicka en fax** _shihk·a ehn fax_
send a package (overnight)	**skicka ett paket (med expressutdelning)** _shihk·a eht pa·keet (meed ehx·prehs·eut·deel·nihng)_

For Communications, see page 49.

Traveling with Children

ESSENTIAL

Is there a discount for kids?	**Har ni barnrabatt?** _hahr nee bahrn·rah·bat_
Can you recommend a babysitter?	**Kan du rekommendera en barnvakt?** _kan deu reh·koh·mehn·dee·ra ehn bahrn·vakt_
Could I have a highchair?	**Kan jag få en barnstol, tack?** _kan yahg foa ehn bahrn·stoal tak_
Where can I change the baby?	**Var kan jag byta på babyn?** _vahr kan yahg bew·ta poa bai·been_
Where's...?	**Var ligger...?** _vahr lih·gehr..._
the amusement park	**nöjesfältet** _nury·ehs·fehl·teht_
the arcade	**arkadhallen** _ar·kahd·ha·lehn_
the kiddie [paddling] pool	**barnbassängen** _bahrn·ba·sehng·ehn_
the park	**parken** _park·kehn_
the playground	**lekplatsen** _leek·plats·ehn_
the zoo	**djurparken** _yeur·park·ehn_
Are kids allowed?	**Får man ta barnen med?** _foar man tah bahr·nehn meed_
Is it safe for kids?	**Är det barnsäkert?** _air det bahrn·sair·kert_

YOU MAY HEAR...

Vad gullig! *vahd <u>geul</u>•ig*	How cute!
Vad heter han/hon? *vahd <u>hee</u>•tehr han/hoan*	What's his/her name?
Hur gammal är han/hon? *heur <u>gam</u>•al air han/hoan*	How old is he/she?

Out & About

Can you recommend something for kids?	**Kan du föreslå något för barn?** *kan deu furr•reh•s<u>loa</u> <u>noa</u>•goht furr bahrn*
Where's...?	**Var är...?** *Vahr air...*
the amusement park	**nöjesparken** *nuy•ehs•pahr•kehn*
the arcade	**gallerian** *gah•le•ree•an*
the kiddie [paddling] pool	**barnbassängen/plaskdammen** *bah•rn•ba•sehng•ehn/plask•da•mehn*
the park	**parken** *par•kehn*
the playground	**lekplatsen** *lehk•plat•sehn*
the zoo	**djurparken** *yeur•par•kehn*
Are kids allowed?	**Tillåts barn?** *tihl•oats bahrn*
Is it safe for kids?	**Är det säkert för barn?** *air deht seh•kehrt furr bahrn*
Is it suitable for... year olds?	**Passar det för...-åringar?** *<u>pas</u>•ar dee furr... <u>oa</u>•rihng•ar*

For Numbers, see page 179.

Baby Essentials

Do you have…?	**Har ni…?** *hahr nee…*	
a baby bottle	**en nappflaska** *ehn nap·flas·ka*	
baby food	**babymat** *behy·bih·maht*	
baby wipes	**våtservetter för barn** *voat·ser·veht·er furr·bahrn*	
a car seat	**en bilbarnstol** *ehn beel·bahrn·stoal*	
a children's menu	**en barnmeny** *ehn bahrn·meh·new*	
a children's portion	**en barnportion** *bahrn·pohrt·shoan*	
a highchair	**en barnstol** *ehn bahrn·stoal*	
a crib	**en barnsäng** *ehn bahrn·sehng*	
diapers [nappies]	**blöjor** *blury·ohr*	
formula	**välling** *vehl·ihng*	
a pacifier [dummy]	**en napp** *ehn nap*	
a playpen	**ett lekrum** *eht leek·ruhm*	
a stroller [pushchair]	**en sittvagn** *ehn siht·vangn*	
Can I breastfeed the baby here?	**Får jag amma barnet här?** *foar yahg ah·ma bahr·neht hair*	
Where can I change the baby?	**Var kan jag byta på babyn?** *vahr kan yahg bew·ta poa bai·been*	

For Dining with Children, see page 64.

Babysitting

Can you recommend a reliable babysitter?	**Kan du rekommendera en pålitlig barnvakt?** *kaun deu re·koh·mehn·dee·rahra ehn poa·leet·lihg bahrn·vakt*
What's the charge?	**Vad kostar det?** *vahd kos·tar dee*
We'll be back by…	**Vi kommer tillbaka** *Vee koh·mehr tihl·bah·ka*
I'll pick them up at…	**Jag hämtar dem…** *yahg hehm·tar dehm…*
I can be reached at…	**Du kan nå mig på…** *deu kan noa may poa…*

For Time, see page 181.

Health & Emergency

Can you recommend a pediatrician?	**Kan du rekommendera en barnläkare?** *kan deu reh·koh·men·dee·ra ehn bahrn·lairk·a·rer*
My child is allergic to...	**Mitt barn är allergiskt mot...** *miht bahrn air a·lehr·gisk moat...*
My child is missing.	**Mitt barn har kommit bort.** *miht bahrn hahr koh·miht bohrt*
Have you seen a boy/girl?	**Har du sett en pojke/flicka?** *hahr deu seht ehn poy·ker/flih·ka*

For Meals & Cooking, see page 65.

For Health, see page 166.

For Police, see page 164.

Disabled Travelers

ESSENTIAL

Is there...?	**Finns det...?** *fihns det...*
access for the disabled	**ingång för rörelsehindrade** *in·goang furr rur·rehl·seh·hihn·dra·der*
a wheelchair ramp	**en rullstolsramp** *ehn reul·stoals·ramp*
a handicapped- [disabled-] accessible toilet	**en handikappanpassad toalett** *ehn hand·ee·kap·an·pas·ad toa·ah·leht*
I need...	**Jag behöver...** *yahg beh·hur·ver...*
assistance	**hjälp** *yehlp*
an elevator [lift]	**en hiss** *ehn hihs*
a ground floor room	**ett rum på bottenvåningen** *eht ruhm poa boh·tehrn·voa·nihng·hen*

Asking for Assistance

I'm disabled.	**Jag är handikappad.** *yahg air <u>hand</u>•ee•kap•ad*
I'm deaf.	**Jag är döv.** *yahg air d**u**rv*
I'm visually/hearing impaired.	**Jag är synskadad/hörselskadad.** *yahg air <u>sewn</u>•skah•dad/<u>hur</u>•sel•<u>skah</u>•dad*
I'm unable to walk far/use the stairs.	**Jag kan inte gå långt/gå i trappor.** *yahg kan <u>ihn</u>•ter g**oa** loangt/g**oa** ee <u>trap</u>•ohr*
Can I bring my wheelchair?	**Kan jag ta med min rullstol?** *kan yahg tah meed mihn <u>ruhl</u>•st**oa**l*
Are guide dogs permitted?	**Är det tillåtet med ledarhund?** *air dee tihl•<u>loa</u>•teht meed <u>leed</u>•ar•huhnd*
Can you help me?	**Kan du hjälpa mig?** *kan deu yehl•pa may*
Could you open/hold the door?	**Kan du öppna/hålla upp dörren?** *kan deu urp•na/<u>hoa</u>•la uhp <u>dur</u>•rehn*

In an Emergency

Emergencies

ESSENTIAL

Help!	**Hjälp!** *yelp*
Go away!	**Ge er iväg!** *yeh ehr ee·vairg*
Stop thief!	**Stoppa tjuven!** *stop·a shcheu·vehn*
Get a doctor!	**Hämta en läkare!** *hehm·ta ehn lair·ka·rer*
Fire!	**Det brinner!** *dee brihn·ehr*
I'm lost.	**Jag har gått vilse.** *yahg hahr goat vihl·ser*
Can you help me?	**Kan du hjälpa mig?** *kan deu yehl·pa may*

YOU MAY HEAR...

Fyll i blanketten, tack. *fewl ee blan·keht·ehn tak*
Please fill out this form.

Er legitimation, tack. *ehr lehg·ee·tih·ma·shoan tak*
Your identification, please.

När/Var hände det? *nair/vahr hehn·dehr dee*
When/Where did it happen?

Hur ser han/hon ut? *hewr seer han/hoan eut*
What does he/she look like?

ESSENTIAL

Call the police!	**Ring polisen!** *rihng poa·lee·sehn*
Where's the nearest police station?	**Var ligger närmaste polisstation?** *vahr lih·gehr nair·mas·ter poo·lees·sta·shoan*
There's been an accident.	**Det har hänt en olycka.** *det hahr hehnt ehn oa·lewk·a*
I've been attacked.	**Jag har blivit anfallen.** *jahg hahr blee·viht an·fa·lehn*
My child is missing.	**Mitt barn har kommit bort.** *miht bahrn hahr koh·miht bohrt*
I need...	**Jag behöver...** *yahg beh·hur·vehr...*
an interpreter	**en tolk** *ehn tohlk*
to contact my lawyer	**kontakta min advokat** *kohn·tak·ta mihn ad·voh·kaht*
to make a phone call	**ringa ett samtal** *rihng·a eht sam·tahl*
I'm innocent.	**Jag är oskyldig.** *yahg air oa·shewl·dihg*

Crime & Lost Property

I want to report...	**Jag vill anmäla...** *yahg vihl an·mair·la...*
a mugging	**ett överfall** *eht ur·vehr·fal*
a rape	**en våldtäkt** *ehn vohld·tehkt*
a theft	**ett rån** *eht roan*
I've been robbed/ mugged.	**Jag har blivit rånad/överfallen.** *yahg hahr blee·viht roa·nad/ur·veh·fal·ehn*
I've lost...	**Jag har tappet...** *yahg hahr tah·pat...*

My...has been stolen.	**Någon har stulit...**	_noa_•gohn hahr _steu_•liht...
backpack	**min ryggsäck**	mihn _rewg_•sehk
bicycle	**min cykel**	mihn _sew_•kehl
camera	**min kamera**	mihn _kah_•meh•ra
rental car	**min bil/hyrbil**	mihn beel/_hewr_•beel
computer	**min dator**	mihn _dah_•tohr
credit cards	**mina kreditkort**	mee•na kre•_deet_•koart
jewelry	**mina smycken**	mee•na _smew_•ken
money	**mina pengar**	mee•na _pehng_•ar
passport	**mitt pass**	miht pas
purse [handbag]	**min portmonnä**	mihn pohrt•mo•_nai_
traveler's checks [cheques]	**mina resecheckar**	_mee_•na _ree_•seh•shehk•ar
wallet	**min plånbok**	mihn _ploan_•boak
I need a police report for my insurance.	**Jag behöver en polisanmälan till min försäkring.**	yahg beh•hu•vehr ehn poal•ees•an•mailan tihl meen furr•sehk•rihng
Where is the British/ American/Irish embassy?	**Var ligger den brittiska/amerikanska ambassaden?**	var ligger den brittiska/ amerikanska ambassaden?

Health

ESSENTIAL

I'm sick [ill].	**Jag är sjuk.** *yahg air sheuk*
I need an English-speaking doctor.	**Jag behöver en engelsktalande läkare.** *yahg beh-hur-vehr ehn ehng-ehlsk-tahl-an-der lair-ka-rer*
It hurts here.	**Det gör ont här.** *dee yurr oant hair*
I have a stomachache.	**Jag har ont i magen.** *yahg hahr oant ee mah-gehn*

Finding a Doctor

Can you recommend a doctor/dentist?	**Kan du rekommendera en läkare/tandläkare?** *kan deu reh-koh-mehn-dee-ra ehn lair-ka-rer/ tand-lair-ka-rer*
Can the doctor come to see me here?	**Kan doktorn komma och undersöka mig här?** *kan dohk-torn koh-ma ohk eun-der-sur-ka may hair*
I need an English-speaking doctor.	**Jag behöver en engelsktalande läkare.** *yahg beh-uv-ehr en eeng-ehlsk-tah-lan-de leh-ka-re*
What are their office hours?	**Vilka är deras öppettider?** *vihl-ka air dee-ras ur-peh-tee-dehr*
Can I make an appointment for…?	**Kan jag boka en tid…?** *kan yahg boa-ka ehn teed…*
today	**idag** *ee-dahg*
tomorrow	**imorgon** *ee-mo-ron*
as soon as possible	**så snart som möjligt** *soa snahrt som mury-ligt*
It's urgent.	**Det är brådskande.** *dee air broas-kan-der*

Symptoms

I'm...	**Jag...** *yahg...*
bleeding	**blöder** _blur_-dehr
constipated	**är förstoppad** air furr-_stop_-ad
dizzy	**har yrsel** hahr _ewr_-sehl
nauseous	**mår illa.** moar _ihl_-la
vomiting	**kräks.** krairks
It hurts here.	**Det gör ont här.** dee yurr oant hair
I have...	**Jag har...** yahg hahr...
an allergic reaction	**en allergisk reaktion** ehn a-lehr-_gihsk_ ree-ak-_shoan_
chest pain	**ont i bröstet** oant ee _brurs_-teht
cramps	**kramper** kram-pehr
diarrhea	**diarré** dee-ar-ee
an earache	**ont i örat** oant ee _ur_-rat
a fever	**feber** _fee_-behr
pain	**ont** oant
a rash	**ett utslag** eht _eut_-slahg
a sprain	**en stukning** ehn _steuk_-nihng
some swelling	**en lätt svullnad** ehn leht _sveul_-nad
a stomachache	**ont i magen** oant ee _mah_-gehn
sunstroke	**solsting** _soal_-stihng
I've been sick [ill] for...days.	**Jag har varit sjuk i...dagar.** yahg hahr _vah_-riht sheuk ee..._dah_-gar

For Numbers, see page 179.

Conditions

I'm anemic/diabetic.	**Jag är anemisk/diabetiker.** yahg air a-_nee_-mihsk/ dee-a-_beh_-tih-ker
I'm epileptic.	**Jag har epilepsi** yahg hahr eh-pih-leh-psi
I'm allergic to antibiotics/penicillin.	**Jag är allergisk mot antibiotika/penicillin.** yahg air a-lehr-_gihsk_ moat an-tih-bee-_oa_-tee-ka/pehn-eh-si-_leen_

YOU MAY HEAR...

Vad är det för fel? *vahd air dee fur feel*
What's wrong?

Var gör det ont? *vahr yur dee oant*
Where does it hurt?

Gör det ont här? *yur deht ohnt hehr*
Does it hurt here?

Tar du någon annan medicin? *tahr deu noa·gohn an·an meh·dih·seen*
Are you taking any other medication?

Är du allergisk mot något? *air deu a·lehr·gihsk moat noa·goht*
Are you allergic to anything?

Öppna munnen. *urp·na muhn·ehn*
Open your mouth.

Andas djupt. *an·das yeupt*
Breathe deeply.

Hosta, tack. *hoas·ta, tak*
Cough, please.

Du behöver åka till sjukhuset. *deu beh·hur·vehr oa·ka tihl sjeuk·heu·seht*
You need to go to the hospital.

I have...	**Jag har...** *yahg hahr...*
arthritis	**artrit** *ar·treet*
asthma	**astma** *as·ma*
high/low blood pressure	**högt/låg blodtryck** *hurgt/loagt bload·trewk*
a heart condition	**hjärtproblem** *yairt·proa·bleem*
I'm taking... (medicine).	**Jag tar...(medicin).** *yahg tahr... (meh·dee·seen)*

Treatment

Can you prescribe a generic drug [unbranded medication]?	**Kan du skriva ut ett generiskt läkemedel [generika]?** *Kahn deu skrih·va eut eht gehn·eh·rih·skt lai·keh·meh·dehl [gehn·eh·rih·ka]*
Where can I get it?	**Var hittar jag det?** *vahr hih·tar yahg deht*

Do I need a prescription/ medicine?	**Behöver jag ett recept/medicin?** *beh·hur·vehr yahg eht reh·sehpt/meh·dih·sihn*

For Pharmacy, see page 171.

Hospital

Please notify my family.	**Var snäll och underrätta min familj.** *vahr snehl ohk eun·der·rehta mihn fa·mily*
I'm in pain.	**Jag har ont.** *yahg hahr oant*
I need a doctor/nurse.	**Jag behöver en läkare/sjuksköterska.** *yahg beh·hur·vehr ehn lair·ka·rer/sheuk·shur·ter·ska*
When are visiting hours?	**När är det besökstid?** *nair air dee beh·surks·teed*
I'm visiting…	**Jag vill besöka…** *yahg vihl beh·sur·ka…*

Dentist

I've broken a tooth/lost a filling.	**Jag har brutit av en tand/tappat en plomb.** *yahg hahr breu·tiht afv ehn tand/tap·at ehn plohmb*
This tooth hurts.	**Den här tanden gör ont.** *dehn hair tan·dehn yur oant*
Can you fix this denture?	**Kan du reparera den här tandprotesen?** *kan deu reh·pa·ree·ra dehn hair tand·proh·tees·ehn*

Gynecologist

I have menstrual cramps/a vaginal infection.	**Jag har mens värk/en vaginal infektion.** *yahg hahr mens vehrk/ehn va·gih·nahl ihn·fehk·shoan*
I missed my period.	**Min mens har inte kommit.** *mihn mehns hahr ihn·ter koh·miht*
I'm on the Pill.	**Jag tar p-piller.** *yahg tahr pee·pihl·ler*
I'm (…months) pregnant.	**Jag är (…månader) gravid.** *Yahg air (…moh·na·dehr) gra·veed*
I'm (not) pregnant.	**Jag är (inte) gravid.** *yahg air (ihn·ter) gra·veed*

I haven't had my period for... months.	**Jag har inte haft mens på... månader.** yahg hahr <u>ihn</u>•ter haft mehns poa...<u>**moa**</u>•na•dehr

For Numbers, see page 179.

Optician

I've lost...	**Jag har tappat...** yahg hahr <u>tap</u>•at...
a contact lens	**en kontaktlins** ehn kohn•<u>takt</u>•lihns
my glasses	**mina glasögon** <u>mee</u>•na <u>glahs</u>•<u>ur</u>•gohn
a lens	**en lins** ehn lihns

Payment & Insurance

How much does it cost?	**Hur mycket kostar det?** heur <u>mew</u>•ker <u>kos</u>•tar dee
Can I pay by credit card?	**Kan jag betala med kreditkort?** kan yahg beh•<u>tah</u>•la meed kreh•<u>deet</u>•koart
I have insurance.	**Jag har försäkring.** yahg hahr furr•<u>sair</u>•krihng
Can I have a receipt for my insurance?	**Kan jag få ett kvitto för mitt försäkringsbolag?** kan yahg **foa** eht <u>kvih</u>•toh furr miht furr•<u>sair</u>•krihngs•boa•lahg

Pharmacy

ESSENTIAL

Where's the nearest pharmacy?	**Var är närmaste apotek?** *vahr air nair·mas·teh a·poa·teek*
What time does the pharmacy open/close?	**När öppnar/stänger apoteket?** *nair urp·nar/ stehng·ehr a·poa·tee·keht*
What would you recommend for...?	**Vad kan du rekommendera för...?** *vahd kan deu reh·koh·mehn·dee·ra furr...*
How much should I take?	**Hur mycket ska jag ta?** *heur mew·ker skah yahg tah*
Can you fill [make up] this prescription for me?	**Kan ni göra iordning det här receptet åt mig?** *kan nee yur·ra ee oard·nihng det hair reh·sehp·teht oat may*
I'm allergic to...	**Jag är allergisk mot...** *yahg air a·lehr·gihsk moat...*

In addition to filling prescriptions, **apotek** (pharmacies) sell over-the-counter medication as well as their own brands of toiletries and cosmetics. Almost all pharmacies are open on weekdays, but not all are open late in the evening or on weekends. Business hours vary considerably depending on the pharmacy. Generally, business hours are between 9:00 a.m. and 5:00 p.m. on weekdays. Locations with evening hours usually close around 9:00 p.m., and weekend hours are generally 10:00 a.m. to 4:00 p.m.

What to Take

How much should I take?	**Hur mycket ska jag ta?** heur <u>mew</u>·ker skah yahg tah
How many times a day should I take it?	**Hur många gånger om dagen ska jag ta det?** heur <u>moang</u>·a <u>goang</u>·er ohm <u>dah</u>·gehn skah yahg tah d**ee**
Is it suitable for children?	**Är det lämpligt för barn?** air d**ee** <u>lehmp</u>·lihgt fu**rr** bahrn
I'm taking... (medicine).	**Jag tar...(medicin).** yahg tahr... (meh·dee·<u>seen</u>)
Are there side effects?	**Ger det några biverkningar?** yehr d**ee** no**a**·gra <u>bee</u>·vehrk·nihng·ar
I'd like some medicine for...	**Jag behöver medicin mot...** yahg beh·<u>hur</u>·vehr meh·dih·<u>seen</u> mo**a**t...
a cold	**en förkylning** ehn fu**rr**·<u>chewl</u>·nihng
a cough	**hosta** <u>hoas</u>·ta
diarrhea	**diarré** dee·a·<u>reh</u>
a headache	**huvudvärk** huh·vuhd·vairk
an insect bite	**ett insektbett** eht in·<u>sekt</u>·beht
motion sickness	**åksjuka** <u>oak</u>·sheu·ka

YOU MAY SEE...

EN GÅNG/TRE GÅNGER PER DAG	once/three times a day
TABLETTER	tablets
DROPPAR TESKEDAR	drop teaspoons
FÖRE/EFTER/TILLSAMMANS MED MÅLTIDER	before/after/with meals
PÅ FASTANDE MAGE	on an empty stomach
SVÄLJS HELA	swallow whole
KAN ORSAKA DÅSIGHET	may cause drowsiness
ENDAST FÖR UTVÄRTES BRUK	for external use only

a sore throat	**halsont** <u>hals</u>·oant
a sunburn	**solbränna** <u>soal</u>·brehn·a
a toothache	**tandvärk** tand·vairk
an upset stomach	**ont i magen** oant ee <u>mah</u>·gehn

Basic Supplies

I'd like...	**Jag skulle vilja ha...** yahg <u>skuh</u>·ler <u>vihl</u>·ya hah...
acetaminophen [paracetamol]	**acetominofen** a·seht·a·mihn·oa·<u>fehn</u>
antiseptic cream	**antiseptisk salva** an·tih·<u>sehp</u>·tihsk sal·va
aspirin	**huvudvärkstabletter** <u>heu</u>·vuhd·vairks·ta·<u>bleh</u>·ter
bandage [plasters]	**gasbinda** <u>gahs</u>·bihn·da
a comb	**kam** kam
condoms	**kondomer** kohn·<u>doa</u>·mehr
contact lens solution	**kontaktlinsvätska** kohn·<u>takt</u>·lins·veht·ska
deodorant	**deodorant** dee·oa·deh·<u>rant</u>
a hairbrush	**en hårborste** ehn <u>hoar</u>·bohrsh·ter
hair spray	**hårspray** <u>hoar</u>·spray
ibuprofen	**ibuprofen** ee·beu·proa·<u>fehn</u>
insect repellent	**myggolja** <u>mewg</u>·ohl·ya

a nail file	**en nagelfil**	*ehn nah·gehl·feel*
a (disposable) razor	**en (engångs)-rakhyvel**	*ehn (een·goangs)·rahk·hew·vehl*
razor blades	**rakblad**	*rahk·blahd*
sanitary napkins [towels]	**bindor**	*bin·dohr*
shampoo/	**schampo**	*sham·poa*
conditioner	**hårbalsam**	*hoar·bal·sam*
soap	**tvål**	*tvoal*
sunscreen	**solskyddskräm**	*soal·shewds·krairm*
tampons	**tamponger**	*tam·poang·ehr*
tissue	**papper näsdukar**	*pa·pehrs·nairs·deu·kar*
toilet paper	**toalettpapper**	*toa·a·leht·pa·pehr*
a toothbrush	**tandborste**	*tand·bohr·ster*
toothpaste	**tandkräm**	*tand·krairm*

For Baby Essentials, see page 159.

The Basics

Grammar

Regular Verbs

The present tense of regular verbs in Swedish is formed by adding either -r or -er to the stem. If the stem ends in **a**, add an -**r**, if it ends in a consonant add -**er**. The past tense is formed by adding either -**de** or -**te** to the basic form. If the basic form ends in a **p**, **t**, **k** or **s**, add -**te**, if not then add -**de**. The future is formed by adding the present tense of **ska** (will) + the verb in the infinitive. This applies to all persons (e.g., I, you, he, she, it, etc.). Following are the present, past and future forms of the verbs **att köpa** (to buy) and **att fråga** (to ask). The different conjugation endings are in bold.

	Present	Past	Future
att köpa (to buy)	köp**er**	köp**te**	ska köpa
att fråga (to ask)	fråga**r**	fråga**de**	ska fråga

Pronouns

I	**jag**	it (common/neuter)	**den/det**
you (sing.,inf.)	**du**	we	**vi**
he	**han**	you (pl.)	**ni**
she	**hon**	they	**de**

In Swedish there are two terms for 'you': **du** (singular/informal) and **ni** (plural/informal). Both are used when talking to relatives, friends, colleagues, children, between young people and in work situations. The plural form, **ni**, is used in more formal situations to refer to one or more persons. Its use has however become less frequent, so nowadays you will hear most people address each other with **du**.

Irregular Verbs

There are a number of irregular verbs in Swedish; these must be memorized. Like regular verbs, however, the irregular verb form remains the same, irrespective of person. The table below shows the present, past and future conjugations for a number of important, useful irregular verbs.

	Present	Past	Future
att vara (to be)	**är**	**var**	**ska vara**
att ha (to have)	**har**	**hade**	**ska ha**
att komma (to come)	**kommer**	**kom**	**ska komma**
att göra (to do)	**gör**	**gjorde**	**ska göra**
att gå (to go/walk)	**går**	**gick**	**ska gå**

sing. = singular, inf. = informal, pl. = plural

Word Order

Swedish is similar to English in terms of word order for simple sentences: It follows the subject-verb-object pattern.

Example:

Sara läser en bok. Sara is reading a book.

When the sentence doesn't begin with a subject, the word order changes; the verb and the subject are inverted.

Example:

Nu läser Sara en bok. Now Sara is reading a book.

However, **nu** could just as well be placed at the end of the sentence, e.g. **Sara läser en bok nu.**

Questions are formed by reversing the order of the subject and verb:

| **Du ser katten.** | You see the cat. |
| **Ser du katten?** | Do you see the cat? |

Negations

A statement can be negated by inserting the word **inte** after the verb:

Jag talar svenska.	I speak Swedish.
Jag talar inte svenska.	I do not speak Swedish.

Nouns & Articles

The indefinite article (a, an) is expressed with **en** for common nouns and with **ett** for neuter nouns. Generally, common nouns can be both feminine and masculine (e.g. people, animals, etc.); neuter nouns have no gender (e.g. house, roof, etc.). However, there are several exceptions to this rule.

In Swedish, there are five different endings used to form plural nouns; three correspond to common gender nouns and two to neuter gender nouns. The following rules apply to nouns in the indefinite singular.

1. **en** words that end in -**a** take an -**or** ending
2. **en** words that end in -**e** take an -**ar** ending
3. **en** words with stress on the last vowel take an -**er** ending
4. **ett** words that end in a vowel take an -**n** ending
5. **ett** words that end in a consonant take no additional ending

Common gender nouns that end in a consonant are not covered by the rules above. These words will take either an -**ar** ending or an -**er** ending. The nouns which fall into this category will simply need to be memorized.

Singular indefinite	Plural indefinite
en flicka (a girl)	**flickor**
en timme (an hour)	**timmar**
en telefon (a telephone)	**telefoner**
ett konto (an account)	**konton**
ett hus (a house)	**hus**
en bil (a car)	**bilar**

Definite articles: where in English we say 'the car', the Swedes say the equivalent of 'car-the', i.e. they tag the definite article onto the end of the noun. In the singular, common nouns take an **-en** ending, neuter nouns an **-et** ending. In the plural, common nouns add an **-na** and neuter nouns take an **-en** ending, neuter nouns an **-et** ending. In the plural, common nouns add an **-na** and neuter nouns take an **-en**.

	Singular	**Plural**
common gender	**katten** the cat	**katterna** the cats
neuter gender	**tåget** the train	**tågen** the trains

Demonstrative Adjectives

	Common	**Neuter**	**Plural**
this/these	**denna**	**detta**	**dessa**
that/those	**den**	**det**	**de**
	denna bil	**detta hus**	
	(this car)	(this house)	

Possessive Adjectives

	Common	**Neuter**	**Plural**
my	**min**	**mitt**	**mina**
your (sing.)	**din**	**ditt**	**dina**
our	**vår**	**vårt**	**våra**
his	**hans**		
hers		**hennes**	
its		**dess/dess**	
their		**deras**	
your (pl.)	**er**	**ert**	**era**

Adverbs & Adverbial Expressions

Adverbs are generally formed by adding **-t** to the corresponding adjective.

Hon går snabbt. She walks quickly.

Snabb quick

Numbers

ESSENTIAL

0	**noll**	*nohl*
1	**ett**	*eht*
2	**två**	*tvoa*
3	**tre**	*tree*
4	**fyra**	*few•ra*
5	**fem**	*fehm*
6	**sex**	*sehx*
7	**sju**	*sheu*
8	**åtta**	*oh•ta*
9	**nio**	*nee•oa*
10	**tio**	*tee•oa*
11	**elva**	*ehl•va*
12	**tolv**	*tohlv*
13	**tretton**	*treh•tohn*
14	**fjorton**	*fyeur•tohn*
15	**femton**	*fehm•tohn*
16	**sexton**	*sehx•tohn*
17	**sjutton**	*sheu•tohn*
18	**arton**	*ar•tohn*
19	**nitton**	*nih•tohn*
20	**tjugo**	*shcheu•goa*
21	**tjugoett**	*shcheu•goa•eht*

22	**tjugotvå** _shcheu_·goa·tv**oa**
30	**trettio** _treh_·tee·oa
31	**trettioett** _treh_·tee·oa·eht
40	**fyrtio** _fuhr_·tee·oa
50	**femtio** _fehm_·tee·oa
60	**sextio** _sehx_·tee·oa
70	**sjuttio** _sheu_·tee·oa
80	**åttio** _oh_·tee·oa
90	**nittio** _nih_·tee·oa
100	**hundra** _huhn_·dra
101	**hundraett** _huhn_·dra·eht
200	**två hundra** _tvoa_ huhn·dra
500	**fem hundra** _fehm_ huhn·dra
1,000	**ett tusen** eht _teu_·sehn
10,000	**tio tusen** _tee_·oa _teu_·sehn
1,000,000	**en miljon** ehn mihl·**yoan**

Ordinal Numbers

first	**första** _furs_·ta
second	**andra** _an_·dra
third	**tredje** _tree_·dyer
fourth	**fjärde** _fyair_·der
fifth	**femte** _fehm_·ter
once	**en gång** ehn goang
twice	**två gånger** tvoa _goang_·ehr
three times	**tre gånger** tree _goang_·ehr

Time

ESSENTIAL

What time is it?	**Hur mycket är klockan?** *heur _mew_•ker air _kloh_•kan*
It's noon [midday].	**Klockan är tolv.** *_kloh_•kan air tolv*
Midnight.	**Midnatt.** *_meed_•nat*
From 9 o'clock	**Från nio till sjutton.** *froan _nee_•oa tihl*
to 5 o'clock.	*sheu•_tohn_*
It's twenty after [past] four.	**Den är tjugo över fyra.** *dehn air _shcheu_•goa ur•ver _few_•ra*
It's a quarter to nine.	**Den är kvart i nio.** *dehn air kvart ee _nee_•oa*
5:30 a.m.	**Halv sex på morgonen.** *_halv_ sehx poa _mor_•oh•nehn*
5:30 p.m.	**Halv sex på kvällen.** *_halv_ sehx poa _kveh_•lehn*

Sweden officially follows the 24-hour clock. Formal
communication, such as public transporation schedules and
TV programming, follows this system. However, in ordinary
conversation, time is generally expressed as shown above, often with
the addition of **på morgonen** (in the morning), **på förmiddagen**
(mid-morning), **på eftermiddagen** (in the afternoon), **på kvällen**
(in the evening) and **på natten** (at night).

Days

ESSENTIAL

Monday	**måndag**	_moan_·dahg
Tuesday	**tisdag**	_tees_·dahg
Wednesday	**onsdag**	_oans_·dahg
Thursday	**torsdag**	_toash_·dahg
Friday	**fredag**	_free_·dahg
Saturday	**lördag**	_lurr_·dahg
Sunday	**söndag**	_surn_·dahg

Dates

yesterday	**igår**	ee·_goar_
today	**idag**	ee·_dahg_
tomorrow	**imorgon**	ee·_mo_·ron
day	**dag**	dahg
week	**vecka**	_veh_·ka
month	**månad**	_moa_·nad
year	**år**	_oa_r

Months

January	**januari**	ya·neu·_ah_·ree
February	**februari**	fehb·reu·_ah_·ree
March	**mars**	mash
April	**april**	ap·_rihl_
May	**maj**	maiy
June	**juni**	_yeu_·nee
July	**juli**	_yeu_·lee
August	**augusti**	a·_guhss_·tee
September	**september**	sehp·_tehm_·behr

October	**oktober** *ohk•toa•behr*
November	**november** *noh•vehm•behr*
December	**december** *dee•sehm•behr*

Sweden follows a day-month-year format instead of the month-day-year format used in the U.S.
E.g.: July 25, 2008; **25/07/08** = 7/25/2008 in the U.S.

Seasons

spring	**vår** *voar*
summer	**sommar** *soh•mar*
fall [autumn]	**höst** *huhst*
winter	**vinter** *vihn•tehr*

Holidays

January 1, New Year's Day **Nyårsdagen**
January 6, Epiphany **Trettondagen**
May 1, May Day **Första maj**
June 6, Flag Day **Flaggans dag**
December 25, Christmas Day **Juldagen**
December 26, Boxing Day **Annandag jul**
Moveable dates include:

Good Friday	**Långfredagen**
Ascension	**Kristi himmelfärdsdag**
Whitsunday	**Pingstdagen**
All Saints' Day	**Allhelgonadagen**
Midsummer Day	**Midsommardagen**

The two most important holidays in Sweden are Midsummer and Christmas. **Midsommardagen** (Midsummer) is celebrated with midsummer poles (similar to the may pole) and traditional songs and dances. Traditional food includes **matjesill** (pickled herring), fresh fish and schnapps. For **Juldagen** (Christmas), special cakes and other delicious treats are prepared, such as **pepparkakor** (ginger cookies), **saffranbullar** (saffron buns) and **julbord** (Christmas **smörgåsbord,** a festive buffet). Though not an official holiday, **Luciadagen** (St. Lucia Day) on December 13 marks the beginning of the Chirstmas season. Swedes also celebrate the beginning of spring on April 30, which is known as **Valborgsmässoafton,** with huge bonfires, fireworks and singing. June 6 is **Flaggans dag** (Flag Day), the national day of Sweden. Streets are decorated with yellow and blue, the colors of the Swedish flag, patriotic speeches are made and traditional games and meals are enjoyed.

Conversion Tables

When you know	Multiply by	To find
ounces	28.3	grams
pounds	0.45	kilograms
inches	2.54	centimeters
feet	0.3	meters
miles	1.61	kilometers
square inches	6.45	sq. centimeters
square feet	0.09	sq. meters
square miles	2.59	sq. kilometers
pints (U.S./Brit)	0.47/0.56	liters
gallons (U.S./Brit)	3.8/4.5	liters
Fahrenheit	5/9, after 32	Centigrade
Centigrade	9/5, then +32	Fahrenheit

Kilometers to Miles Conversions

1 km	0.62 miles
5 km	3.1 miles
10 km	6.2 miles
50 km	31 miles
100 km	62 miles

Measurement

1 gram	**gram** _khrahm_	= 0.035 oz.
1 kilogram (kg)	**kilogram** _kee·loa·khrahm_	= 2.2 lb
1 liter (l)	**liter** _lee·tuhr_	= 1.06 U.S./ 0.88 Brit. quarts
1 centimeter (cm)	**centimeter** _sehn·tee· may·tuhr_	= 0.4 inch
1 meter (m)	**meter** _may·tuhr_	= 3.28 feet
1 kilometer (km)	**kilometer** _kee·loa·may·tuhr_	= 0.62 mile

Temperature

	- 5° C – 23° F	15° C – 59° F
- 40° C – -40° F	-1° C – 30° F	20° C – 68° F
-30° C – -22° F	0° C – 32° F	25° C – 77° F
-20° C – -4° F	5° C – 41° F	30° C – 86° F
-10° C – 14° F	10° C – 50° F	35° C – 95° F

Oven Temperature

100° C – 212° F	177° C – 350° F
121° C – 250° F	204° C – 400° F
149° C – 300° F	260° C – 500° F

Dictionary

English–Swedish

A

about (approximately) omkring
accept v acceptera
accident olycka
accommodation logi
acetaminophen paracetamol
across över
acupuncture akupunktur
adapter adapter
address n adress
adopt v adoptera
after efter
age ålder
air conditioning luftkonditionering
air mail flygpost
airline flygbolag
airport flygplats
aisle seat plats i mittgången
all alla
allergic allergisk
allergic reaction allergisk reaktion
allergy allergi
allow v tillåta
alter v ändra på
alternate route annan väg

aluminum foil aluminiumfolie
a.m. fm
ambulance ambulans
amount summa
amusement park nöjesfält
and och
anemic anemisk
animal djur
another annan
antiques store antikaffär
antiseptic cream antiseptisk salva
anyone någon
anything något
apartment lägenhet
apologize v be om ursäkt
appliance apparat
approve v godkänna
area code riktnummer
aromatherapy aroma-terapi
arrival ankomst
arrive v anlända
ask v fråga
aspirin huvudvärkstablett
asthma astma
at vid

adj adjective	**BE** British English	**v** verb
adv adverb	**n** noun	

ATM Bankomat
attack *n* anfall
audio guide audioguide
authentic äkta
automatic automatisk
available ledig
away iväg

B

baby baby
baby bottle nappflaska
baby formula välling
baby wipes våtservetter för barn
babysitter barnvakt
backpack ryggsäck
bad dålig
bag (shopping) påse
baggage cart bagagekärra
baggage claim bagageutlämning
bakery bageri
band (music group) band
bandage (gauze) gasbinda
bank bank
bank charge bankavgift
banknote sedel
bar bar
barber herrfrisör
bath bad
bathroom badrum; **(toilet)** toalett
battery batteri
battlefield slagfält

be *v* vara
beach strand
beautiful vacker
become *v* bli
bed *n* säng
before före
begin *v* börja
behind bakom
belt skärp
between mellan
big stor
bicycle cykel
bicycle lock cykelås
bikini bikini
bill *n* **(restaurant bill)** nota; **(hotel, invoice)** räkning
birthday födelsedag
bite *n* bett; *v* **(bite)** bita; *v* **(chew)** tugga
black svart
blanket *n* täcke
bleed *v* blöda
blood blod
blood pressure blodtryck
blouse blus
board *v* **(flight)** borda
boarding house pensionat
boarding pass (airport) boardingkort
boat båt
boat tour båttur

book bok
bookstore bokhandel
boots stövlar
boring trist
botanical garden botanisk trädgård
bottle flaska
bottle opener flasköppnare
bowl djup tallrik
boy pojke
boyfriend pojkvän
bra behå
bracelet armband
break v gå sönder
breakdown v (car) gå sönder
breastfeed v amma
breathe andas
bridge bro
bring ta med
broken (broken) sönder;
  (damaged) trasig
brooch brosch
broom sopborste
brown brun
burn v brinna
bus buss
bus route busslinje
bus station bussterminal
bus stop busshållplats
business center businesscenter
business hours öppettider
business trip affärsresa

busy upptagen
but men
buy v köpa

C

cabin stuga
cafe kafé
calender kalender
call v (phone) ringa
calm lugn
camera kamera
camping bed tältsäng
can n burk; v (be able to) kan
can opener konservöppnare
cancel v avbeställa
car bil
car deck (ferry) bildäck
car ferry bilfärja
car park [BE] parkeringsplats
car rental biluthyrning
car seat bilbarnstol
carafe karaff
card n kort
carry on n (luggage) handbagage
cash kontant
cashier (male) kassör; **(female)**
  kassörska
casino kasino
castle slott
cathedral katedral
cave grotta

cell phone mobiltelefon
ceramics keramik
certificate of authenticity äkthetsbevis
chair lift stollift
change n (money) växel; v (transportation; a baby) byta; v (reservation) ändra;
cheap billig
check in v checka in
check in desk (airport) incheckning
check out v checka ut
checking account checkkonto
chemical toilet kemisk toalett
chemist [BE] apotek
chest bröstet
child barn
child's cot [BE] barnsäng
children's menu barnmeny
church kyrka
cigar cigarr
cinema [BE] bio
city (city) stad; (downtown) centrum
city map stadskarta
classical music klassiskmusik
clean n ren
cleaning supplies städutrustning
clear v (computer) rensa
cliff klippa
cling film [BE] plastfolie

clock klocka
close v stänga
closed stängt
clothing store klädaffär
coat rock
coffee shop konditori
coin mynt
cold (illness) förkylning; (temperature) kall
colleague kollega
color färg
comb kam
come v komma
company (business) firma; (companionship) sällskap
computer dator
concert konsert
conditioner hårbalsam
condom kondom
conference konferens
conference room konferensrum
confirm v (reservation) bekräfta
contact lens solution kontaktlinsvätska
contain v innehålla
contraceptive preventivmedel
convention hall kongresshall
cooking facilities kokmöjligheter
cool (temperature) sval
copy n kopia
copy machine kopieringsautomat

corkscrew korkskruv
correct rätt
cost v kosta
cotton bomull
cough n hosta; v hosta
country code landsnummer
cover charge kuvertavgift
credit card kreditkort
crib barnsäng
cross country skiing längdåkning
crystal (glass) kristallglas
cup kopp
culture kultur
currency valuta
currency exchange office
   växelkontor
customs tull
customs declaration form
   tulldeklaration
cute adj gullig
cycling cykelåkning

D

dala horse dalahäst
damage v (damage) skada; n
   (harm) skada
dance v dansa
dance club diskotek
day ticket dagsbiljett
day trip dagstur
deaf döv

debit card bankkort
declare v (customs) förtulla
deck chair solstol
deep djup
delay n försening
delete v (computer) radera
delicatessen delikatessaffär
denim denim
dentist tandläkare
denture tandprotes
deodorant deodorant
depart v (train) avgå
department store varuhus
departure (airport) avgång
departure gate avgångsgate
deposit handpenning
desire adj gärna; n lust
detour trafikomläggning
develop v (photos) framkalla
diabetic n diabetiker
dial v (number) slå
diamond diamant
diaper blöja
diarrhea diarré
diesel diesel
difficult svårt
digital digital
digital print digitalt kort
dirty smutsig
disabled rörelsehindrad
disabled accessible toilet [BE]

handicappanpassad toalett
discount rabatt
discount card rabattkort
dish detergent diskmedel
dishwasher diskmaskin
display case vitrin
disposable camera engångskamera
disturb v störa
dive v dyka
divide v dela
diving equipment dykarutrustning
divorced skild
dizzy yr
do v (do something) göra; (work with) syssla med
do not disturb var god stör ej
doctor doktor
doll docka
dollar dollar
domestic (travel) inrikes
domestic flight inrikes flyg
domestic partner sambo
door dörr
dosage dosering
downtown centrum
dress klänning
dress code klädsel
drive v köra
driver's license körkort
drops (medication) droppar
dry cleaner kemtvätt

dubbed dubbad
duty free taxfri
duty free good taxfri vara

E

each varje
ear öra
earring örhänge
east öster
easy lätt
eat v äta
economy class turist klass
electrical outlet nätuttag
elevator hiss
e-mail e-post
e-mail address e-postadress
emergency nödsituation
emergency brake nödbroms
emergency exit nödutgång
English engelska
engrave v gravera
enter n (entrance) ingång; (computer) enter
entertainment underhållning
equipment utrustning
escalator rulltrappa
e-ticket e-biljett
European Union (EU) europeiska unionen
event händelse
examine v (medical) undersöka

excess baggage överviktsbagage
exchange rate växelkursen
excuse me (attention, pardon)
  ursäkta; **(to get past)** ursäkta mig
exit n **(way out)** utgång
expensive dyr
expert avancerad
express express
express mail expresspost
extension (phone) anknytning
eyeglasses glasögon

F

fabric tyg
family familj
fan (ventilation) fläkt
fantastic adj fantastisk
fare biljettpris
farm bondgård
fast fort
fax fax
fax machine fax machine
female kvinna
ferry färja
fever feber
field fält
fill v **(prescription)** göra i ordning
filling (dental) plomb
film [BE] film
fire exit brandutgång
first första

fishing fiske
fit v **(clothing)** passa
fitting room provrum
fix v laga
fixed price fast pris
flat [BE] lägenhet
flight flyg
flight number flygnummer
floor (level) våning
football [BE] fotboll
for (someone) för
foreign currency utländsk valuta
forest skog
forget v glömma
fork gaffel
form n blankett
fountain fontän
free (available) ledig
free of charge gratis
freezer frys
friend vän
from ifrån
frying pan stekpanna
fun rolig
function v **(work)** fungera
further (more) ytterligare

G

game spel
garbage sopor
garbage bag soppåse

gasoline bensin
gas station bensinstation
gate (boarding) gate
genuine äkta
get off (train) stiga av
gift shop presentaffär
gift present
girlfriend flickvän
give v ge
glass (drinking) glas
gold guld
golf golf
golf club golfklubba
golf course golfbana
good adj bra
goodbye hej då
greengrocer [BE] livsmedelsaffär
grocery store livsmedelsaffär
group grupp
guest gäst
guide (brochure) guide; (person) guide
guide dog ledarhund
gym gym

H

hair cut klippning
hair dryer hårtork
hair style frisyr
hairbrush hårborste
hairdresser damfrisör

hairspray hårspray
half halv
handbag [BE] handväska
handicapped rörelsehindrade
handicapped accessible toilet handicappanpassad toalett
handicraft hantverk
handmade handgjord
hat hatt
have v ha
health food store hälsokostaffär
hearing impaired hörselskadad
heat värme
helmet hjälm
help n hjälp; v hjälpa
here här
hi hej
highchair barnstol
highway motorväg
hike v vandra
hiking vandring
hill kulle
hire v [BE] rent
holiday [BE] (vacation) semester
holiday (celebration) helgdag
horseback riding ridsport
hospital sjukhus
hot varm
hotel hotell
hour timme
husband man

I

ibuprofen ibuprofen
ice hockey ishockey
identification (idenitification) legitimation; **(ID card)** ID-kort
ill [BE] sjuk
in i
included (in the price) inkluderad
indoor pool inomhusbassäng
information desk information
innocent oskyldig
insect insekt
insect bite insektbett
insect repellent mygg olja
inside inuti
instant messenger instant messenger
instructor instruktör
insurance försäkring
interesting intressant
international (travel) utrikes
international driver's license internationellt körkort
internet internet
internet cafe internetkafé
interpreter tolk
iron n **(clothes)** strykjärn; v **(clothes)** stryka
itemized bill specificerad räkning

J

jacket jacka
jeans jeans
jet ski jetski
jeweler juvelerare
jewelry smycken
job jobb

K

keep v behålla
key nyckel
key card nyckelkort
kiddie pool barnbassäng
kiss v kyssa
kitchen kök
knife kniv
krona (Swedish currency) krona

L

lace spets
lactose intolerant laktosinterant
ladies' restroom damtoilett
ladieswear damkläder
lake sjö
last sista
late sen
launderette [BE] snabbtvätt
laundromat snabbtvätt
laundry tvätt
laundry detergent tvättmedel
laundry facilities tvättmöjligheter

lawyer advokat
leather läder
leave v lämna
left (direction) vänster
lesson lektion
letter brev
library bibliotek
life boat livbåt
life jacket flytväst
lifeguard livräddare
lift (ski) lift
lift [BE] n **(elevator)** hiss
lift pass liftkort
light (lamp) lampa
light bulb glödlampa
lighter tändare
like v gilla
line (bus) linje
linen linne
live v bo
loafers loafers
lock v låsa
log on logga in
log out logga ut
long adj lång; adv länge
lose v **(lost luggage)** förlora; v
  (drop, lose) tappa
lost n vilse
lost property office [BE]
  hittegodsexpedition
lost and found hittegodsexpedition

lottery lotto
love v älska
luggage locker förvaringsskåp

M

mail post
mailbox postlåda
manager chef
manicure manikyr
many många
map karta
market marknad
married gift
mass mässan
match (fire) tändsticka
meal måltid
mean v **(signify)** betyda
measuring spoon måttsked
medicine medicin
medium medium
meet v träffa
meeting sammanträde
memory card minneskort
men's restroom herrtoalett
menstrual cramps mensvärk
menstruation mens
menswear herrkläder
menu meny
message meddelande
microwave mikrovågsugn
minimum minimum

Miss fröken
mistake misstag
mobile phone [BE] mobiltelefon
moment ögonblick
mop n skurmop
moped moped
mosque moské
motel motell
motion sickness åksjuka
motorboat motorbåt
motorcycle motocykel
motorway [BE] motorväg
mountain berg
mouth mun
movie film
movies bio
Mr. herr
Mrs. fru
mugging överfall
multi-day card flerdagskort
museum museum
must måste

N

nail file nagelfil
nail salon nagelvårdssalong
name n namn
napkin servett
nappy [BE] blöja
nature reserve naturreservat
nearby nära

necklace halsband
need v behöva
new ny
newspaper tidning
newsstand tidningskiosk
next nästa
next to bredvid
nice adj snäll
no (not allowed) ej
nobody ingen
no smoking rökning förbjuden
north norr
not inte
not included (in the price) inte
  inkluderad
nothing inget
number nummer
nurse sjuksköterska

O

off av
old gammal
on (switch) på
one way (street) enkelriktad
one-way ticket enkel biljett
only bara
open n öppet; v öppna
opening hours [BE] öppettider
opera opera
opposite mitt emot
optician optiker

or eller
orchestra orkester
order *v* beställa
other andra
outdoor utomhus
outdoor pool utomhusbassäng
outside ute
overnight delivery (mail)
  expressutdelning
oxygen treatment syrebehandling

P

pacifier napp
package paket
paddling pool [BE] barnbassäng
pajamas pyjamas
panorama panorama
pants byxor
panty hose strumpbyxor
paper napkin papperservett
parcel [BE] paket
park *n* park; *v* parkera
parking parkering
parking lot parkeringsplats
passport pass
passport control passkontroll
password (computer) lösenord
pay phone telefonautomat
pay *v* betala
peak (mountain) top
pearl pärla

pedestrian crossing
  övergångsställe för fotgängare
pedestrian fotgängare
pedicure pedikyr
pen kulspetspenna
per per
per day per dag
per week per vecka
performance (music, theater)
  föreställning
person person
petite petit
petrol [BE] bensin
petrol station [BE] bensinstation
pewter tenn
pharmacy apotek
phone call samtal
phone card telefonkort
phone number telefonnummer
photo foto
pick up *v* **(person/thing)** hämta
picnic area picknickområde
piece bit
pill tablett
pillow kudde
PIN PIN kod
pink rosa
piste [BE] spår
place *n* ställe
plan *n* plan
plaster [BE] plåster

plastic wrap plastfolie
platform (train) plattform
platinum platina
plate tallrik
play *n* **(theater)** teaterpjäs; *v* spela
playground lekplats
playpen lekrum
pleasant trevlig
please (request) snälla;
  (invitation) varsågod
plunger vaskrensare
pocket *n* ficka
point of interest sevärdhet
police polis
police report polisrapport
police station polisstation
pond damm
post office postkontor
postage porto
postcard vykort
pot (cooking pot) gryta; **(saucepan)**
  kastrull
pound sterling engelsk pund
pregnant gravid
premium (gas) premium
prescription recept
price pris
print (computer) skriva ut
private privat
private room privatrum
problem problem

produce store matbutik
program (events) program
pub pub
public transportation allmänna
  kommunikationer
pull dra
purple lila
purpose syfte
purse (large) handväska, **(small)**
  portmonnä
push tryck
pushchair [BE] sittvagn

R

racket (tennis) racket
railroad järnväg
railway [BE] järnväg
rain regn
raincoat regnkappa
rap rap
rape *n* våldtäkt
rapids fors
rash *n* utslag
(disposable) razor (engångs)
  rakhyvel
reach *v* nå
read *v* läsa
ready färdig
receipt kvitto
receive *v* ta emot
receptionist receptionist

recommend v rekommendera
refrigderator kylskåp
region region
regular gas vanlig
relationship (romantic)
  förhållande
rent n hyra; v hyra
repair v reparera
repairs (car) reparationer
repeat v upprepa
report v **(crime)** anmäla
reservation bokning
reserved reserverad
rest area rastplats
restroom (sign) WC
restaurant restaurang
return v **(give back)** återlämna
return ticket [BE] retur **(biljett)**
reverse charge call [BE] ba- samtal
right (correct) rätt; **(direction)**
  höger
ring (jewelry) ring
river flod
road väg
road map vägkarta
romantic romantisk
room rum
room service rumservice
round n **(golf)** runda
round-trip ticket retur biljett
rubbish [BE] sopor

S

safe n kassaskåp
sailing segling
sandals sandaler
sanitary napkin binda
saucepan kastrull
sauna bastu
save v **(collect)** spara
scarf halsduk
schedule tidsschema
scissors sax
sea hav
seat (on train) plats
seat number platsnummer
seat reservation (train)
  sittplatsbiljett
seminar seminarium
send v skicka
separated (couple) separerad
service serveringsavgift
service charge (bank)
  expeditionsavgift
sex sex
shampoo shampoo
sheet lakan
shoe store skoaffär
shoes skor
shopping basket shoppingkorg
shopping cart shoppingvagn
shopping centre [BE]
  shoppingcenter

shopping mall shoppingcenter
shorts shorts
show v visa
shower dusch
sick sjuk
side effect biverkning
sightseeing tour sightseeingtur
sign v undertäckna
silk siden
SIM card (cell phone) SIM kort
single ticket [BE] enkel **(biljett)**
sit v sitta
size storlek
skiing skidåkning
skirt kjol
slice n skiva
slippers tofflor
slippery (icy) hal
slow adj långsam
small liten
sneakers träningsskor
snorkeling equipment
  snorkelutrustning
snow snö
snowboard snowboard
snowshoes pjäxor
soap tvål
soccer fotboll
sock socka
something något
soon snart

soother [BE] napp
sore throat halsont
sorry förlåt
south söder
souvenir souvenir
spa spa
spatula stekspade
speak v tala
spoon sked
sports massage träningsmassage
spouse (female) maka; **(male)**
  make
sprain stukning
square (town feature) torg
stadium stadion
stair trappa
stamp n frimärke
stamp your ticket stämpla er biljett
start v **(car)** starta
stay n stanna
steakhouse stekhus
steep brant
stolen stulen
stomach magen
stomachache ont i magen
stop n **(bus stop)** bushållplats; v
  stanna
store n butik; v förvara
strange konstig
stream å
street gata

stroller sittvagn
student studerande
study *v* läsa
stunning jättesnygg
subtitle text
suburb förort
subway tunnelbana
subway station tunnelbanestation
suitable lämplig
suitcase resväska
sunburn solbränna
sunglasses solglasögon
sunstroke solsting
super [BE] (gas) premium
supermarket snabbköp
surfboard surfbräda
sweater tröja
sweatshirt sweatshirt
Swedish *adj* svensk; **(language)**
svenska
swelling svullnad
swim *v* simma
swimming pool simbassäng
swimming trunks badbyxor
swimsuit baddräkt
symbol (computer) tecken
symphony (orchestra) symfoni
synagogue synagoga

T

table bord

tablecloth duk
take *v* ta
take out *v* ta ut
taken (occupied) upptagen
tampon tampong
tax skatt
taxi taxi
teaspoon tesked
temperature temperatur
temple tempel
tennis tennis
tennis court tennisbana
terminal (airport) terminal
terrible förskräcklig
text message sms
textiles textil
thank you tack
theft rån
thief tjuv
think *v* tänka
ticket biljett
ticket machine biljettautomat
ticket office biljettkontor
tie *n* slips
tights [BE] strumpbyxor
timetable [BE] tidsschema
tip (service) dricks
tissue näsduk
to till
tobacconist tobaksaffär
toilet [BE] toalett; **(sign)** WC

toilet paper toalettpapper
tooth tand
toothbrush tandborste
toothpaste tandkräm
tour tur
tourist turist
tourist attraction turistattraktion
tourist information
  turistinformation
tourist office turistbyrå
town hall stadshus
toy store leksaksaffär
track (railroad) spår
trail spår
train *n* tåg
train station järnvägsstation
tram spårvagn
translate *v* översätta
travel *v* **(travel)** resa; **(drive)** åka
travel agency resebyrå
travel agent (female)
  resebyråkvinna; **(male)**
  resebyråman
travel sickness [BE] åksjuka
traveler's check resecheck
traveller's cheque [BE] resecheck
treat *v* **(to a meal)** bjuda
trim (hair) putsning
trip *n* resa
trolley [BE] bagagekärra
trouser [BE] byxor

try *v* prova
turn off *v* stänga av
turn on *v* sätta på

U

ugly ful
umbrella (standard) paraply; **(sun)**
  solparasol
underground [BE] tunnelbana
underground station [BE]
  tunnelbanestation
understand *v* förstå
underwear (general) underkläder
unfortunately tyvärr
United Kingdom Storbritanien
unlimited (mileage) obegränsad
until tills
urgent brådskande
United State Förenta Staterna
use *v* använda
username användarnamn
utensil bestick

V

vacancy ledigt rum
vacation semester
vacuum cleaner dammsugare
vaginal infection vaginal infektion
valley dal
valuable värdesak
value *n* värde

vegetarian vegetarian
viewpoint utsiktspunkt
village by
visit n besök; v besöka
visiting hours besökstid
visitor besökare
visitor besökare
visually impaired syn skadad
vomit v kräkas

W

wait vänta
wake up v vakna
wake-up call telefonväckning
walk n promenad; v gå
wallet plånbok
want v vilja
washing machine tvättmaskin
waterfall vattenfall
weather forecast väderleksrapport
weekend helg
welcome välkommen
west väster
wheelchair rullstol
wheelchair ramp rullstolsramp
when när
where var
which vilken
white vitt
who vem

widow änka
widower änkling
window fönster
window seat fönsterplats
windsurfing vindsurfa
wireless internet trådlös internet
with med
withdrawal (bank) uttag
wood trä
wool ull
work from home v arbeta hemifrån
wrap v (present) slå in
write v skriva
wrong fel

Y

yellow gul
yes ja
yield lämna företräde
youth hostel vandrarhem

Z

zoo djurpark

Swedish–English

A

acceptera v accept
adapter adapter
adoptera v adopt
adress n address
advokat lawyer
affärscentrum shopping mall
  [centre BE]
affärsresa business trip
akupunktur acupuncture
alla all
allergi allergy
allergisk allergic
allergisk reaktion allergic reaction
**allmänna
kommunikationer** public
  transportation
alternativ väg alternate route
aluminiumfolie aluminum foil
ambulans ambulance
amma v breastfeed
andas breathe
andra other
anemisk anemic
anfall n attack
anknytning extension (phone)
ankomst arrival
anlända v arrive
anmäla v report (crime)

annan another
antikaffär antiques store
antiseptisk salva antiseptic cream
använda v use
användarnamn username
apotek pharmacy [chemist BE]
apparat appliance
arbeta hemifrån v work from home
armband bracelet
aroma-terapi aromatherapy
astma asthma
audioguide audio guide
automatisk automatic
av off
avancerad expert
avbeställa v cancel
avgå v depart (plane)
avgång departure
avgångsgate departure gate

B

baby baby
bad bath
badbyxor swim trunks
baddräkt swim suit
badrum bathroom [toilet BE]
bagagekärra baggage cart
  [trolley BE]
bagageutlämning baggage claim

bageri bakery
bakom behind
band band (music group)
bank bank
bankavgift bank charge
bankkort debit card
Bankomat ATM
bar bar
bara only (just)
barn child
barnbassäng kiddie pool [paddling pool BE]
barnmeny children's menu
barnstol highchair
barnsäng crib [child's cot BE]
barnvakt babysitter
bastu sauna
batteri battery
be om ursäkt v apologize
behå bra
behålla v keep
behöva v need
bekräfta v confirm (reservation)
bensin gasoline [petrol BE]
bensinstation gas station [petrol station BE]
berg mountain
bergklättring rock climbing
bestick utensil
beställa v order
besök n visit

besöka v visit
besökare visitor
besökstid visiting hours
betala v pay
bett n bite
betyda mean (signify)
bibliotek library
bikini bikini
bil car
bilbarnstol car seat
bildäck car deck (ferry)
bilfärja car ferry
biljett ticket
biljettautomat ticket machine
biljettkontor ticket office
biljettpris fare
billig cheap
bilsäte car seat
biluthyrning car rental
binda sanitary napkin [towel BE]
bio movies [cinema BE]
bit piece
bita v bite
biverkning side effect
bjuda v treat (to a meal)
blankett n form
bli v become
blod blood
blodtryck blood pressure
blus blouse
blöda bleed

blöja diaper [nappy BE]
bo v live
boardingkort boarding pass
bok book
bokhandel bookstore
bokning reservation (travel, restaurant)
bomull cotton
bondgård farm
bord table
borda v board (flight)
botanisk trädgård botanical garden
bra adj good
brandutgång fire exit
brant steep
bredvid next to
brev letter
brinna v burn
bro bridge
brosch brooch
brun brown
brådskande urgent
bröstet chest
burk n can
businesscenter business center
buss bus
busshållplats bus stop [request stop BE]
busslinje bus route
bussterminal bus station
butik n store

by village
byta v change (baby, connection)
byxor pants [trouser BE]
båt boat
båttur boat tour
börja v begin

C

centrum downtown
checka in check in (airport)
checka ut check out (hotel)
chef manager
cigarr cigar
cykel bicycle
cykelåkning cycling
cykelås bicycle lock

D

dagsbiljett day ticket
dagstur day trip
dal valley
dalahäst dala horse
damfrisör hairdresser
damkläder ladieswear
damtoalett ladies' restroom
damm pond
dammsugare vacuum cleaner
dansa v dance
dator computer
dela divide
delikatessaffär delicatessen

denim denim
deodorant deodorant
diabetiker *n* diabetic
diamant diamond
diarré diarrhea
diesel diesel
digital digital
digitalt kort digital print
diskmedel dish detergent
diskmaskin dishwasher
djup deep
djup tallrik bowl
djur animal
djurpark zoo
docka doll
doktor doctor
dollar dollar
dosering dosage
dra pull
dricks tip (service)
droppar drops (medication)
dubbad dubbed
duk table cloth
dusch shower
dyka *v* dive
dykarutrustning diving equipment
dyr expensive
dålig bad
dörr door
döv deaf

E

e-biljett e-ticket
efter after
ej no (do not...)
eller or
endast only (nothing but)
engelska English
engelsk pund pound sterling
engångskamera disposable camera
enkel biljett one-way trip [single ticket BE]
enkelriktad one way (street)
enter enter (computer)
e-post e-mail
e-postadress e-mail address
europeiska unionen European Union (EU)
expeditionsavgift service charge (bank)
express express
expresspost express mail
expressutdelning overnight delivery (mail)

F

familj family
fantastisk *adj* fantastic
fast pris fixed price
fax fax
fax machine fax machine
feber fever

fel wrong
ficka *n* pocket
film movie [film BE]
fiske fishing
flaska bottle
flasköppnare bottle opener
flerdagskort multi-day card
flickvän girlfriend
flod river
flyg flight
flygbolag airline
flygnummer flightnumber
flygplats airport
flygpost airmail
fläkt fan
fm a.m.
fontän fountain
fors rapids
fort fast
fotboll soccer [football BE]
fotgängare pedestrian
foto photo
framkalla *v* develop (photos)
fri free
frimärken stamps
frisyr hair style
fru Mrs.
frys freezer
fråga ask
från from…
fröken Miss

ful ugly
fungera *v* function (work)
fylla *v* fill
fält field
färdig ready
färg color
färja ferry
födelsedag birthday
fönster window
fönsterplats window seat
för tung/stor too much, excess (baggage)
före before
Förenta Staterna United States
föreställning performance (music, theater)
förhållande relationship (romantic)
förlora *v* lose
förlåt sorry
försening *n* delay
förskräcklig terrible
förskylning cold (sick)
första first
förstå *v* understand
försäkring insurance
förtulla *v* declare (customs)
förvaringsskåp luggage locker
förort suburb

G

gaffel fork

gammal *adj* old, *n* age
gasbinda bandage (gauze)
gata street
gate gate (boarding)
ge *v* give
gift married
gilla *v* like
glas glass (drinking)
glasögon eyeglasses
glödlampa light bulb
glömma *v* forget
godkänna *v* approve
golf golf
golfbana golf course
golfklubb golf club
gratis free of charge
gravera *v* engrave
gravid pregnant
grotta cave
grupp group
gryta pot (cooking)
guide guide (brochure); guide (person)
gul yellow
guld gold
gullig *adj* cute
gym gym
gå *v* walk, leave
gå sönder break; breakdown (car)
gärna *adj* desire
göra *v* do

ha *v* have
hal slippery (icy)
halsband necklace
halsduk scarf
halsont sore throat
halv halv
handbagage carry on
handgjord handmade
handicappanpassad toalett handicapped accessible toilet [disabled BE]
handpenning deposit
handväska purse [hand bag BE]
hantverk handicraft
hatt hat
hav sea
hej hi
hej då goodbye
helg weekend
helgdag holiday (celebration)
hemifrån work from home
hemlagad homemade (food)
herr Mr.
herrfrisör barber
herrkläder menswear
herrtoalett men's restroom
iss elevator [lift BE]
hittegodsexpedition lost-and-found [lost property office BE]
hjälm helmet

hjälp *n* help
hjälpa *v* help
hosta *n* cough; *v* to cough
hotell hotel
huvudvärkstablett aspirin
hyra rent [hire BE]
hårbalsam conditioner
hårborste hairbrush
hårspray hairspray
hårtork hair dryer
hälsokostaffär health food store
hämta *v* pick up (thing/person)
händelse event
här here
höger right (direction)
hörselskadad hearing impaired

I

i in
ibuprofen ibuprofen
ID-kort identification
ifrån from
incheckning check in desk (airport)
information information desk
ingen nobody (sg)
inget nothing
ingång entrance
inkluderad included (in the price)
innehålla contain
inomhusbassäng indoor swimming pool

inrikes domestic (travel)
inrikes flyg domestic flight
insekt insect
insektbett insect bite
instant messenger instant messenger
instruktör instructor
inte not
inte inkluderad not included (in the price)
internationellt körkort international driver's license
internet internet
internetkafé internet café
intressant interesting
inuti inside
ishockey ice hockey
iväg away

J

ja yes
jacka jacket
jeans jeans
jetski jet ski
jobb job
juvelerare jeweler
järnväg railroad [railway BE]
järnvägsstation train station
jättesnygg stunning

K

kafé café
kalender calendar
kall cold (temperature)
kam comb
kamera camera
kan v can (be able to)
karaff carafe
karta map
kasino casino
kassaskåp n safe
kassör cashier (male)
kassörska cashier (female)
kastrull saucepan (cooking)
katedral cathedral
kemisk toalett chemical toilet
kemtvätt dry cleaner
keramik ceramics
kjol skirt
klassiskmusik classical music
klippa cliff
klippning hair cut
klocka(n) clock
klädaffär clothing store
klädsel dress code
klänning dress
kniv knife
kokmöjligheter cooking facilities
kollega colleague
komma v come
konditori coffee shop

kondom condom
konferens conference
konferensrum conference room
kongresshall convention hall
konsert concert
konservöppnare can opener
konstig strange
kontaktlinsvätska contact lens solution
kontant n cash
kopia n copy
kopieringsautomat copy machine
kopp cup
korkskruv corkscrew
kort n card, adj short
kosta v cost
kostym suit (jacket/pants)
kreditkort credit card
kristallglas crystal (glass)
krona krona (Swedish currency)
kräkas v vomit
kudde pillow
kulle hill
kulspetspenna pen
kultur culture
kuvertavgift cover charge
kvinna female
kvitto receipt
kylskåp refrigerator
kyrka church
kyssa v kiss

kök kitchen
köpa v buy
köra drive
körkort driver's license

L

laga v fix
lakan sheet
laktosintolerant lactose intolerant
lampa light (lamp)
landsnummer country code
ledarhund guide dog
ledig available
ledigt rum vacancy
legitimation identification
lekplats playground
lekrum playpen
leksaksaffär toy store
lektion lesson
liftkort liftpass
lila purple
linje line
linne linen
liten small
livbåt life boat
livräddare lifeguard
livsmedelsaffär grocery store [greengrocer BE]
loafers loafers
logga in log on (connect to internet)
logga ut log out

logi accommodation
lotto lottery
luftkonditionering air conditioning
lugn calm
lust n desire
lyft lift (ski)
lång long
långsam slow
låsa v lock
läder leather
lägenhet apartment [flat BE]
lämna v leave
lämna före träde yield
lämplig suitable
längdåkning cross country skiing
länge long (time)
läsa v (book) read; (school) study
lätt easy
lösenord password

M

magen stomach
maka spouse (female)
make spouse (male)
man husband, man
manikyr manicure
marknad market
matbutik produce store (general store) [grocer BE]
med with
meddelande message

medicin medicine
medium medium
mellan between
men but
mens menstruation
mensvärk menstrual cramps
meny menu
mikrovågsugn microwave
minimum minimum (requirement)
minneskort memory card
misstag mistake
mitt emot opposite
mobiltelefon cell phone [mobile phone BE]
moms sales tax [VAT BE]
moped moped
moské mosque
motel motel
motorcykel motorcycle
motorbåt motorboat
motorväg highway [motorway BE]
mun mouth
museum museum
mygg olja insect repellent
mynt coin
måltid meal
många many
måste must
måttsked measuring spoon
mässan mass (catholic)

N

nagelfil nail file
nagelvårdssalong nail salon
namn *n* name
napp pacifer [soother BE]
nappflaska baby bottle
naturreservat nature reserve
norr north
nota bill (restaurant)
nummer number
ny new
nyckel key
nyckelkort key card
nå *v* reach
någon anyone
något anything, something
när when
nära nearby
näsduk tissue
nästa next
nätuttag electrical outlet
nödbroms emergency brake
nödsituation emergency
nödutgång emergency exit
nöjesfält amusement park

O

obegränsad unlimited (mileage)
och and
olycka accident
omkring about (approximately)

ont i magen stomachache
opera opera
optiker optician
orkester orchestra

P

paket package [parcel BE]
panorama panorama
papperservett paper napkin
paracetamol acetaminophen
paraply umbrella
park park
parkering parking
parkering på gatan street parking
parkeringsplats (one or several)
  parking lot [car park BE]
pass passport
passa v fit
passkontroll passport control
pedikyr pedicure
pensionat boarding house
per per
per dag per day
per vecka per week
person person
petit petite
picknickområde picnic area
PIN kod PIN code
pjäxor snowshoes
plan n plan
plastfolie plastic wrap [cling film BE]

platina platinum
plats seat (on train)
plats i mittgången aisle seat
platsnummer seat number
plattform platform (train)
plomb filling
plånbok wallet
pojke boy
pojkvän boyfriend
polis police
polisrapport police report
polisstation police station
porto postage
post mail
postkontor post office
postlåda mail box
premium premium [super BE] (gas)
presentaffär gift shop
present gift
preventivmedel contraceptive
pris price
privat private
privatrum private room
problem problem
program progam (events)
prova v try
provrum fitting room
pub pub
putsning trim (hair)
pyjamas pajamas
på on (switch)

påse bag
pärla pearl

R

rabatt discount
rabattkort discount card
racket racket (tennis)
radera delete (computer)
(engångs)rakhyvel (disposable) razor
rap rap
rastplats rest area
recept prescription
receptionist receptionist
region region
regn rain
regnkappa raincoat
rekommendera *v* recommend
ren adj clean
rensa clear (computer, ATM), clean
reparationer repairs (car)
reparera *v* repair
resa *v* travel, *n* trip
resebyrå travel agency
resebyråkvinna travel agent (female)
resebyråman travel agent (male)
resecheck traveler's check [traveller's cheque BE]
reserverad reserved
restaurang restaurant

resväska suitcase
retur (biljett) round-trip ticket [return ticket BE]
ridsport horseback riding
riktnummer area code
ring ring (jewelry)
ringa *v* call (phone)
rock coat
rolig fun
romantisk romantic
rosa pink
rullstol wheelchair
rullstolsramp wheelchair ramp
rulltrappa escalator
rum room
rumservice room service
runda *v* round (golf)
ryggsäck backpack
rån theft
räkning bill (hotel, invoice)
rätt correct
rökning förbjuden no smoking
rörelsehindrad disabled

S

sambo domestic partner
sammanträde meeting
samtal phone call
sandaler sandals
sax scissors
sedel banknote

segling sailing
semester vacation
seminarium seminar
sen late
separerad separated (couple)
serveringsavgift service
servett napkin
sevärdhet point of interest
sex sex
shampoo shampoo
shoppingcenter shopping mall
  [shopping centre BE]
shoppingkorg shopping basket
shoppingvagn shopping cart
shorts shorts
siden silk
sightseeingtur sightseeing tour
simbassäng swimming pool
SIM kort SIM card (cell phone)
simma *v* swim
sista last
sitta *v* sit
sittplatsbiljett seat reservation
  (train)
sittvagn stroller [pushchair BE]
sjuk sick [ill BE]
sjukhus hospital
sjuksköterska nurse
sjö lake
skada *n* damage, *v* harm
skatt tax

sked spoon
skicka *v* send
skidåkning skiing
skild divorced
skiva *n* slice
skoaffär shoe store
skog forest
skor shoes
skriva write
skriva ut print
skurmop *n* mop
skyldig innocent
skärp belt
slagfält battlefield
slips tie
slott castle
slå *v* (phone number) dial
slå in *v* wrap (present)
sms text message
smutsig dirty
smycken jewelry
snabbköp supermarket
snabbtvätt Laundromat
  [launderette BE]
snart soon
snorkelutrustning snorkeling
  equipment
snowboard snowboard
snäll *adj* nice
snälla (request) please
snö snow

socka sock
solbränna sunburn
solglasögon sunglasses
solsting sunstroke
solstol deck chair
sopborste broom
sopor garbage (garbage disposal) [rubbish BE]
soppåse garbage bag
souvenir souvenir
spa spa
spara v save
specifierad räkning itemized bill
spel game
spela v play
spets lace
spår trail [piste BE]; track (railroad)
spårvagn tram
stad city
stadion stadium
stadshus town hall
stadskarta city map
stanna n stay; v stop
starta v start
stekhus steakhouse
stekpanna frying pan
stekspade spatula
stiga av get off (train)
stollift chair lift
stor big
Storbritannien United Kingdom

storlek size
strand beach
strumpbyxor panty hose [tights BE]
strykjärn iron (clothes)
studerande student
stuga cabin
stukning n sprain
stulen stolen
städutrustning cleaning supplies
ställe place
stämpla er biljett stamp your ticket
stäng av turn off
stänga v close
stängt closed
störa disturb
stövlar boots
summa amount
surfbräda surfboard
sval cool (temperature)
svart black
sweatshirt sweatshirt
svensk adj swedish
svenska adj swedish; (language) Swedish
svullnad swelling
svårt difficult
syfte purpose
symfoni symphony (orchestra)
syn skadad visually impaired
synagoga synagogue
syrebehandling oxygen treatment

syssla med v do (work with)
sällskap company (companionship)
säng bed
sätta på turn on
söder south
sönder broken

T

ta v take
ta emot v receive
ta med bring
ta ut take out
tablett pill (tablet)
tack thank you
tala v speak
tallrik plate
tampong tampon
tand tooth
tandborste toothbrush
tandkräm toothpaste
tandläkare dentist
tandprotes dentures
tappa v lose; drop
taxfri duty free
taxfri vara duty free good
taxi taxi
teaterpjäs play (theater)
tecken symbol (computer)
telefon katalog telephone catalog
telefonautomat pay phone
telefonkort phone card

telefonnummer phone number
telefonväckning wake up call
temperatur temperature
tempel temple
tenn pewter
tennis tennis
tennisbana tennis court
terminal terminal (airport)
tesked teaspoon
text subtitle
textil textiles
tidning newspaper
tidningskiosk newsstand
tidsschema schedule [timetable BE]
till to
tills until
tillåta v allow
timme hour
toalett bathroom [toilet BE]
toalettpapper toilet paper
tobaksaffär tobacconist
tofflor slippers
tolk interpreter
top peak (moutain)
torg square (town feature)
trappa stair
trasig broken (damaged)
trevlig pleasant
trist boring
tryck push
trådlös internet wireless internet

trä wood
träffa v meet
träfigur wood carvings
träkniv wooden knife
träningsmassage sports massage
träningsskor sneakers
träsked wooden spoon
träskor wooden clogs
tröja sweater
tugga v chew
tull customs
tulldeklaration customs declaration form
tunnelbana subway [underground BE]
tunnelbanestation subway station [underground station BE]
tur tour
turist tourist
turist klass economy class
turistattraktion tourist attraction
turistbyrå tourist office
turistinformation tourist information
tvål soap
tvätt laundry
tvättmaskin washing machine
tvättmedel laundry detergent
tvättmöjligheter laundry facilities
tyg fabric
tyvärr unfortunately

tåg train
täcke n blanket
tältsäng camping bed
tändare lighter
tändsticka match (fire)
tänka v think

U

ull wool
underhållning entertainment
underkläder underwear (general)
undersöka v examine (medical)
undertäckna v sign
upprepa v repeat
upptagen busy
ursäkta v excuse me (to get attention, pardon me)
ursäkta mig excuse me (to get past)
ute outside
utgång exit way out
utländsk valuta foreign currency
utomhus outdoor
utomhusbassäng outdoor pool
utrikes international (travel)
utrustning equipment
utsiktspunkt view point
utslag n rash
uttag withdrawal (bank)

V

vacker beautiful

vaginal infektion vaginal infection
vakna v wake up
valuta currency
vandra v hike
vandrarhem youth hostel
vandring hiking
vanlig regular gas
var where
var god stör ej do not disturb
vara v be
varje each
varm hot
varsågod (invitation) please
varuhus department store
vaskrensare plunger
vattenfall waterfall
WC (sign) restroom [toilet BE]
veckotidning magazine
vegetarian vegetarian
vem who
vid at
vilja v want
vilken which
vilse lost
visa v show
vitrin display case
vitt white
vykort postcard
våldtäkt n rape
våning floor (level, etage in building)
våtservetter för barn baby wipes

väderleksrapport weather forecast
väg road
vägkarta road map
välkommen welcome
välling baby formula
vän friend
vänster left (direction)
vänta wait
värde n value
värdesak n valuable
värme heat
väska bag
väster west
växel n change (money)
växelkontor currency exchange office
växelkursen exchange rate
växla change money

Y

yr dizzy
ytterliggare further (more)

Å

å stream
åka v travel, drive (motor vehicle)
åksjuka motion sickness [travel sickness BE]
ålder age
återlämna v return (give back)
äkta authentic

äkthetsbevis certificate of
  authenticity
älska v love
ändra v change (reservation)
ändra på v alter
änka widow
änkling widower
äta v eat

Ö

ögonblick (one) moment
öppet open
öppettider business hours [opening
  hours BE]
öppna v open
öra ear
öre öre (Swedish currency)
örhänge earring
öster east
över across (the road)
överfall mugging
övergångsställe för fotgängare
  pedestrian crossing
översätta v translate
överviktsbagage excess baggage

speaking your language

**phrase book & dictionary
phrase book & CD**

Available in: Arabic, Cantonese Chinese, Croatian, Czech, Danish, Dutch,
English*, Finnish*, French, German, Greek, Hebrew*, Hindi, Hungarian*,
Indonesian, Italian, Japanese, Korean, Latin American Spanish, Mandarin
Chinese, Mexican Spanish, Norwegian, Polish, Portuguese, Romanian*,
Russian, Spanish, Swedish, Thai, Turkish, Vietnamese

*Book only

www.berlitzpublishing.com